COMPLETE GROUP COUNSELING PROGRAM *for* CHILDREN *of* DIVORCE

Ready-to-Use Plans & Materials for Small & Large Groups, Grades 1-6

SYLVIA MARGOLIN

JOSSEY-BASS
A Wiley Imprint
www.josseybass.com

Published by Jossey-Bass
A Wiley Imprint
989 Market Street, San Francisco, CA 94103-1741   www.josseybass.com

Jossey-Bass books and products are available through most bookstores. To contact Jossey-Bass directly call our Customer Care Department within the U.S. at 800-956-7739, outside the U.S. at 317-572-3986 or fax 317-572-4002.

Jossey-Bass also publishes its books in a variety of electronic formats. Some content that appears in print may not be available in electronic books.

Library of Congress Cataloging-in-Publication Data

Margolin, Sylvia
    Complete group counseling program for children of divorce : ready-to-use plans &
materials for small and large groups, grades 1–6 / Sylvia Margolin.
        p.   cm.
    ISBN 0-87628-124-2
    ISBN 0-7879-6631-2 (layflat)
        1. Children of divorced parents—Counseling of—Handbooks, manuals, etc.   2.
Group counseling for children—Handbooks, manuals, etc.   3. School social work—
Handbooks, manuals, etc.   I. Title.
    HQ777.5.M374   1996
    373.14'6—dc20   96-4054

FIRST EDITION
HB Printing 10 9 8 7 6 5 4

This book is dedicated to my parents
Jack and Perl Samuels
who have been married for over fifty years

and to

my husband Victor and
my daughter Myra.

ACKNOWLEDGMENTS

I would like to acknowledge the contributions of, and to deeply thank the following for their help and inspiration:

My supervising teacher at Campbell Junior High School in New York, Marlene Garnett, for teaching me how to write lesson plans that taught concepts and were also creative and fun.

The former Director of Special Education of the Round Lake Schools, Dr. Rebecca Volkert, for suggesting the structure for topic-specific groups and giving me the freedom to create them.

My friend and colleague, Ellen Sontag, for looking at the artwork done by the students in the case studies and for helping me with "Tips for Parents."

My colleagues from the University of Illinois Social Work School, Kathy Lucas, Carol Henry, and Linda Sandman, for also looking at the artwork done by students in the case studies section.

A teaching assistant, Maria Caro, for helping me with translations into Spanish.

My creative daughter, Myra Margolin, for the delightful artwork.

My husband, Victor Margolin, for encouraging me to extend my expertise to a larger audience, and, as he had already written and edited quite a number of books, for serving as a model.

Connie Kallback of Simon & Schuster for her suggestions and encouragement to make this book a "book."

The trusting and open children who have been in groups over the years, and who shared their experiences with me.

The parents of these children, who confided in me, who expressed appreciation, and who allowed me to reproduce some of the work of their children as case studies.

Divine inspiration for allowing me to receive the idea to create this book.

ABOUT THE AUTHOR

Sylvia Margolin received her B.A. degree from Queens College in New York, her M.A. degree in Education from New York University, and her M.S.W. from the University of Illinois at Chicago, Jane Addams School of Social Work.

Mrs. Margolin was a teacher with preschool, elementary, and middle-school aged children for ten years in public and private schools. After obtaining her M.S.W., she worked as a school social worker for the next eleven years in both elementary and middle schools, doing both individual and group counseling.

As a school social worker, she has led two to four groups a year for children of divorce. She felt the need for a curriculum guide that both addressed the needs and held the interest of the children in the group. Using both her teaching and social work expertise, she created *A Complete Group Counseling Program for Children of Divorce*.

I have led counseling groups for children of divorce every year for the last ten years because there have always been children who have needed help dealing with the separation of their parents. I have worked on and reworked the lesson plans and reproducible activity sheets in the book during each of these years. Not only did I want them to work for groups of younger and older elementary-aged children in both small and large classroom groups, I also wanted to include and address all the issues that arise for children of divorcing parents.

There is an introduction, "Creating Children of Divorce Groups," that describes how to start and then run the counseling group, with ideas for check-ins at the beginning and closings at the end for the sessions. Also included are many of the forms and notices you may need, such as an article for a newsletter to publicize the group's formation, letters to parents and teachers, a permission form, and a questionnaire and information handout for parents. Four of there are also offered in Spanish for the benefit of Spanish-speaking parents.

Following the introduction, the body of the book consists of twelve sessions. These address both the needs of the group, such as introductions and termination, and the various issues children may face:

1. General Background

2. Why Parents Marry and Divorce

3. Changes

4. Two Houses

5. Feeling Angry

6. Feeling Guilty

7. The Grieving Process

8. Legal Issues

9. Stepparenting

10. A Happy Marriage

11. Review

12. Termination: Achieving Closure

For each session (except the eleventh), there is a description of "Background Issues" for the particular topic. My intention was to provide information to group leaders and teachers about the various issues that children in the group may be facing and suggestions regarding what to say in response to the pain or confusion the children may express.

Ready-to-use lesson plans and reproducible activity sheets come after the "Background Issues" for each session. Then, there is a page called "Adaptations," which provides suggestions for modifying the lesson plans for use with nonreaders and nonwriters, with older elementary-aged children, or with whole classroom groups.

After the twelve sessions, there is a section of the book called "Case Studies." The responses and art work of six children are described, analyzed, and reproduced. So much can be gleaned not only from what the children tell you but also from what they show in their art. If you haven't had experience processing artistic input from children, reading the sample case studies should help.

The last section of the book is an appendix. Annotated bibliographies of books and media resources about parents divorcing and remarrying are included. Both the sixth and the ninth lesson plans call for the use of resources from these lists. The appendix also includes a bibliography of references used in writing this book.

I have gotten very positive feedback from children who have been in these groups as well as from many of their parents. I hope that the ideas and activities in *A Complete Group Counseling Program for Children of Divorce* help you so that you, in turn, can help children who are struggling to cope with and accept the changes in their families.

CONTENTS

Creating Groups for Children of Divorce

GETTING STARTED

Each year, as a school social worker, I lead one or more groups for children whose parents are separated or divorced. For some, the separation or divorce is recent, while for others, though the divorce may have occurred at least one year prior to the group's formation, the children still have unresolved issues about it and resist accepting the situation.

I discover who these children are by sending a memo to each teacher in the school and by placing a notice about the group in the school newsletter. Teachers and parents contact me in response to my inquiry.

I telephone the parents of each child referred to tell them what we will be doing in the group, to screen out inappropriate referrals, and to get verbal permission for the child to be included in the group. (Written permission forms are sent home with the children either at this time or at the end of the first session.) In addition, I explain that it is helpful for me to learn a little about the family situation so that I can better understand the child's thoughts and feelings, and, depending on the parent's preference, I do a telephone or in-person interview, or send home the parent questionnaire included in the Forms section of this book.

I generally have between four and ten children in a group, and I try to separate those in grades 1-3 from the older elementary students in grades 4-6. However, when numbers are small, I include students of all grades in the same group. Groups consist of both boys and girls and, because of the universal nature of the topic, this has never posed a problem. I try not to have one of anything in a group, i.e., one boy, one first grader, etc. Each session lasts about 45 minutes.

This program can also be used by teachers or counselors with classroom groups. The focus would shift to learning about different kinds of families rather than only divorced ones. Following each session there are suggested adaptations for using the activity with an entire class.

USING THE PROGRAM

I start every session but the first with a check-in to find out how each group member is feeling and what has happened during the week since the last time we met. At first, I am more directed with the opening question, until the members understand what the check-in is about. I might show a chart of feeling faces (see worksheet following the introduction) and ask each group member in turn to choose the one with which he/she is identifying and tell why. I might ask each to choose one that matches how he/she felt sometime within the last week and tell what happened to make him/her feel that way. I might ask each member to tell one good thing and one bad thing that happened to him/her during the week. I might ask what he/she did over the weekend and to tell about any visit to a noncustodial parent. Another possibility is to ask if the children had any strong thoughts or feelings over the week as a result of the previous week's session. I usually jot down some notes to help me remember key things the children tell me, and then in subsequent sessions I ask them about these specific things. When one person is talking, the others in the group just listen. Sometimes I say, "Does anyone want to ask _____ a question about what he/she said?" In this way, the group members practice listening skills.

The activities included in the lesson plan follow the check-ins. At the end of some sessions, I have included a "Closing" to help end the session on a lighter note. Following the introduction is a list of these and other "Closings" that can be used when there is extra time.

I keep all the papers the children complete on file until the last session when they are stapled into folded large sheets of construction paper and made into a book. These are for the children to take home and share with their parents if they wish.

Following each activity, there is a page called "Adaptations." Included are modifications for nonreaders and writers (both younger children and those in special education classes), for older children aged nine through twelve, and for classroom groups. The items that need adapting are numbered to correspond with the item in the lesson plan for that session.

This group counseling model has proven very beneficial in providing an outlet for children to discuss an issue that is a major concern in their lives. In addition, the children often feel less isolated as they hear about others who have similar plights. In the appendix are case studies of children who have been in groups, and samples of their work are included. When the group is over, the children leave with some issues clarified, with an awareness of others who share their concerns, and with a little more acceptance of their family situation.

FEELING FACES

CLOSINGS

Here are some different ways to end the sessions when time allows. Some have been written into the lesson plans.

1. Knots Game—Have children stand in a circle. With the right hand, each person will hold the hand of any other child in the group except for the two people on either side of him/her. Do the same with the left hand. Everyone is now all knotted up. Without letting go of the people's hands, the group members will try to untangle themselves.

2. Anger Scribble—Distribute a sheet of paper and a marker to each child. Have him/her scribble out anger on the paper, pressing hard. Then have each one crush the paper into a ball and throw the "anger" into the trash can.

3. Movement Scribble—Scribble in large circular movements. Then, have the marker jump up and down. Then, have it run back and forth, kick a ball, swing a bat. Then use two colors and have them chase each other.

4. Hand Tower—First child places one hand on the table. The next child places his/her hand on top, and continue around the circle till each child has one hand on the hand tower. Then continue the tower using the other hand of each child. Then, the hand on the bottom is placed on the top of the tower, and this is repeated over and over again.

5. Scribble Picture—Each child scribbles on his/her own sheet of paper with a marker. Pass the sheet to the person on the left. Have that person find pictures, numbers, or letters in the scribble and outline them with a marker of another color.

6. Writing on Backs—Have one child write with his/her finger on the back of another child in the group. The message can be a letter, a number, a shape, and so on.

7. Scary or Angry Drawing—Each child quickly sketches something that he/she feels is scary or that makes him/her angry, then draws something very powerful to destroy it, or tears the picture into tiny pieces and throws it away.

8. Shapes in our Palms—Have each child find a shape in the lines on the palm of another child in the group.

9. Pass-A-Pic—Have each child start a picture. After one minute, pass the picture to the person on the left who continues the picture. Continue until the picture returns to the child who started it. Share.

10. Pass—Stand in a circle. Leader passes around something (a handshake, a tweak on the ear, a pat on the shoulder, etc.) and each person who receives this passes it to the next one until it returns to the leader. Then the leader passes one thing going one way and something else going the other.

11. Counting on Each Other—Have pairs of children stand facing each other, touching palms. Then each child takes a step back. Repeat until the palms no longer touch. Count how many steps each pair was able to take before the palms could no longer touch. Compare.

CLOSINGS, *CONTINUED*

12. Needing Each Other—Pairs of children sit on the floor back-to-back with elbows linked. Without using hands, they must rise to standing position. They need to support each other's backs until both are standing.

PARENT ARTICLE FOR NEWSLETTER

A support group is being formed called Children of Divorce. It will begin on
_____.
Children who have recently experienced parental separation or divorce are welcome to participate. Also, the group may benefit children whose parents have separated or divorced in the past, but who are still struggling to accept it.

The group will meet once each week for approximately forty-five minutes during school hours. There is no fee.

If you are interested, call _____ at
_____ phone number.

LETTER TO TEACHERS

Date: _____

To: _____

From: _____

A support group will soon be started for children whose parents have recently separated or divorced, or for those who are still struggling with parental separation issues. If you are aware of any children in your class who would benefit from such a group, please list their names below. You will be notified about the dates and time the group will be meeting.

Students' Names:

LETTER TO PARENTS

Dear Parents,

A Children of Divorce support group is being formed at _____ School for students in grades _____. The group is open to children who have recently experienced parental separation or to those who still resist accepting the situation. The groups usually consist of four to ten children who have had similar feelings and experiences.

We will cover issues such as changes in the family that occur as a result of divorce, living in two houses, the grieving process, legal issues, and stepparenting. There will be discussion and activities in each session. All the written and art work the children have done will be saved and sent home in book form after the last session. Your child may be interested in sharing this "book" with you.

The group will meet once each week during the regular school day for approximately forty-five minutes. There will be a total of twelve sessions.

If you would like your son or daughter to participate in the group, please fill out the attached Parent Permission Form and have your child return it to me. I have also included a confidential questionnaire. It is not necessary to fill this out, but if your son or daughter will be joining the group, the information asked for helps me to understand the issues with which your child is dealing. I will be the only person to see the responses. The "Tips for Parents" handout is for you to keep. It includes recommendations that hopefully will be helpful to you.

If you have any questions regarding the program, please feel free to contact me by calling _____. I look forward to working with your child and helping him or her through this difficult life experience.

Sincerely,

CARTA A LOS PADRES

Estimados Padres,

El grupo de apoyo a niños de padres divorsiados està formando en la escuela _____ para los estudiantes en los grados _____. El grupo está abierto a los niños que recientemente han experimentado la separación de los padres o a los que todavia se resisten en acceptar la situacion. Los grupos normalmente consisten de cuarto a diez niños que comparten sentimientos y experiencias similares.

Nosotros cubriremos areas como los cambios en la familia que occuren como resultado de divorcio, vivienda en dos casas, el proceso de aceptación, procesos legales, y padrasto o madrastra. Habrán discusiones y actividades en cada sesión. Todo el arte y cosas escritas que los niños han hecho estarán archivados y enviadas a la casa en forma de un libro despues de la ultima sesión. El o ella prodra compartir este "libro" con ustedes si asi lo desea.

El grupo se reunirá una vez cada semana durante el dia escolar por cuarenta y cinco minutos, por un total de doce sesiónes.

Si desea usted que su hijo o hija participe en el grupo, por favor de llenar la forma adjunto (Forma de Autorisación) y devolverla a la escuela con su niño. Tambien esta incluido un questionario confidencial. No es necesario llenarlo, pero si su hijo o hija va a juntarse con el grupo, la informacione me ayudaria a entender los conflictos de su hijo o hija. Yo seré la unica persona a ver la información. El "Recomendaciones A Los Padres," este informe es para que ustedes lo guarda. El informe incluye información que sera de aprovecho para su familia.

Si usted tiene alguna pregunta acerca del programa, por favor sentirse libre de comunicarse a este telefono _____. Yo le anticipo trabajar con su niño y ayudarle con esta experiencia sumamente dificil.

Sinceramente,

FOLLOW-UP LETTER TO PARENTS WHO COULD NOT BE REACHED BY PHONE

Date: _____

Dear _____,

Because I could not reach you by phone, I am writing to inform you of a group I am starting in the school during school hours. The group is for children whose parents have recently separated or divorced, or for children who still have unresolved issues about their parents' separation or divorce even though it occurred a while ago.

Your child's teacher, _____, thought that your son/daughter, _____, would benefit from participating in such a group. If you agree and would like your child included, please sign the attached permission form. I am also enclosing a letter to parents that explains more about the group.

Also included is a confidential questionnaire. It is not necessary to fill this out, but if your son or daughter will be joining the group, the information asked for helps me to understand the issues with which your child is dealing. I will be the only person to see the responses. The "Tips for Parents" handout is for you to keep. It includes recommendations that hopefully will be helpful to you.

You can send the permission form and the questionnaire back to school with your child in a closed envelope to my attention. Your child can give this to the teacher who will get it to me.

If you have any questions, please feel free to call me at _____.

Respectfully,

Sylvia Margolin,
School Social Worker

PARENT PERMISSION FORM

I give my child _____ permission to participate in a Children of Divorce support group. The group will begin on _____ and end approximately twelve weeks later. It will meet once each week during the regular school day for approximately forty-five minutes.

_____
Parent Signature

FORMA DE AUTORIZACION

Mi hijo/hija _____ puede participar en el Grupo de Apoyo a Niños de Padres Divorsiados. El grupo va a commensar el _____ y terminar aproximadamente en doce semanas. Se reunira una vez por semana durante el dia esolar, de cuarenta y cinco minutos.

_____

Firma del Padre ó Guardian

TIPS FOR PARENTS

- Your children need simple explanations about the separation or divorce to help them understand that they were not the cause of it. Tell them in advance when it will happen, why it is happening, and what sort of visitation schedule is being set up.

- Expect children to show signs of grief following the separation or divorce, and let them know you understand. Though at first they may pretend not to care or believe what is happening, soon they will show emotions. Being upset is part of what they must go through.

   Preschoolers generally feel guilty for causing the problems.
   Young elementary-age children usually experience sadness.
   Children over the age of eight or nine most often feel angry.

- Your child will need to be reassured that you love him or her. Children sometimes believe that because parents stop loving each other, they may also someday stop loving the children.

- Children of all ages may act babyish for a while, like baby-talking, bed wetting, having temper tantrums, clinging, and pretending to be ill. In general, they need extra support, not punishment, at this time, to regain their former self-confidence.

- Many changes may occur that children can learn to accept when you explain things to them and continue to be lovingly attentive and firm: less money, less attention, more responsibilities, moving, new school, new friends, new work schedule, different rules and discipline styles in each home.

- Don't argue in front of your child.

- Don't criticize the other parent to your child. Usually, your child loves both of you.

- Don't use your child as a messenger to deliver information to the other parent.

- Don't use your child as a spy to find out what the other parent is doing.

- Don't use your child to get revenge on the other parent by denying child support or visitation.

- Set up a regular visitation schedule. Children feel most secure when they know when and for how long the visitation will occur.

- Even if you live out-of-state, regular contact by phone and/or letter is important to let the child know you still love and care about him or her.

- Don't feel you need to provide special toys, treats, or outings at each and every visit. Children need normal family time in both parents' homes.

- Continue to set rules and limits as you did in the past. Children need this consistency in each home.

- Your child needs to know that your decision to separate or divorce is final. Children tend to fantasize for years after the separation that their parents will reunite.

15

- Meet new dates away from the home at first rather than having many strangers coming and going in your children's lives.

- After divorce, some parents blame themselves for any misbehavior or unhappiness their child experiences. All children go through rough stages in their growth. You don't need to think that it would have been different if only you and your spouse had stayed together.

RECOMENDACIONES A LOS PADRES

- Sus niños necesitan explicaciones simples sobre la separación o divorcio para ayudarlos a comprender que ellos no fueron la causa de el mismo. Digales por adelantado cuando pasará, porque está pasando, y que tipo de horario de visita está planeado.

- Anticipe que los niños mostrarán los signos de dolor por la separación o divorcio, informeles que usted comprende. Aunque al principio ellos pretendan que no les importa o no creen lo que pasa, pronto ellos mostraran emociones. Estar confundidos es algo que ellos deben experimentar.

  Los niños de edad preèscolar generalmente se sienten culpables por lo sucedido y los problemas.

  Los niños (edad elemental) generalmente experimentan la tristeza.

  Niños sobre la edad de ocho o nueve frecuentemente se sienten enfadados.

- Su niño necesitará estar seguro de que usted le ama. Los niños en ocasiones creen que porque los padres se dejan de amar, tambien un día dejaran de amar a los niños.

- Los niños de todas las edades puede actuar como los bebes por un tiempo, orinarse en la cama, teniendo cambios de tenperamento, agárrandose, y pretendiendo estar enfermo. Por regla general, ellos necesitan apoyo y no castigo en ese tiempo, para recobrar su seguridad en si mismo.

- Muchos cambios pueden occurir, los niños pueden aprender acceptar cuando usted le explica cosas a ellos y continua siendo cariñosa (o) y firme; menos dinero, menos atencíon, mas responsabilidades, mudanzas, nueva escuela, nuevos amigos, nuevo horario de trabajo, reglas differentes y estilos de disciplina en cada hogar.

- No discutan en frente de su niño(s).

- No critique el otro padre delante de su niño. Usualmente su niño le ama a ambos.

- No use a su niño como mensajero para entregar informaciones al otro padre.

- No use a su niño como un espia para descubrir lo que haga el otro padre.

- No use a su niño para vengarse contra el otro padre para negar sustento o derechos de visita.

- Arreglar un horario de visita regular. Los niños se sienten mas seguros cuando ellos saben cuando y por cuanto tiempo la visita durará.

- Si usted vive fuera del estado, el contacto regular por telefono y/o carta es importante para comunicar al niño que usted todavia le ama y se preocupa por el o ella.

- No sienta que usted debe proveer juguetes espesiales o regalos en cada visita. Los niños necesitan tiempo normal en ambos hogares.

- Continue poniendo reglas y limites como usted hizo en el pasado. Los niños necesitan esta consistencia en cada hogar.

- Su niño necesita saber que su decision de separarse o divorciarse es definitiva. Los niños tienden a ilusionarse por años despues de la separacion que los padres se volveran a reconsiliar.

- Inicialmente mantenga sus nuevas relaciones fuera de la casa, es mejor que tener muchos estraños entrando y saliendo de las vidas de sus niños.

- Despues del divorcio, algunos padres se culpan por cualquier mala conducta o desdicha que su niño experimenta. Todos los niños pasan por etapas dificiles en su desarollo. Usted no necesita pensar que pudo haber sido diferente si solamente usted y su esposo se hubiesen quedado juntos.

QUESTIONNAIRE FOR PARENTS

Directions: Answer only those questions about which you feel comfortable. The questionnaire will be kept confidential. The group leader will use the answers to gain understanding and sensitivity about your child's situation to better help him or her. Completing this questionnaire is voluntary, and your child will not be excluded from the group if you choose not to fill this out.

CHILD'S NAME _____

CUSTODIAL PARENT'S NAME _____

NONCUSTODIAL PARENT'S NAME _____

1. When did the separation occur?_____

2. Would you mind sharing a little about the reason you and your husband/wife decided to separate? _____
   _____
   _____

3. When and how did you explain the reason for the separation to the children?_____
   _____
   _____
   _____

4. How did the children react immediately afterward? Since the separation?_____
   _____
   _____
   _____

5. Have your children done things that you are aware of to try to get you and your ex-spouse to reunite? _____
   _____
   _____
   _____

6. What arrangements were made for the visitation (how often, where, for what length of time, who picks up and delivers the children)? How are the visitation arrangements working out? _____
   _____
   _____
   _____

7. Are you and your spouse still having major conflicts? Do these pertain to issues about the children, like child support and visitation? Is the child aware of these conflicts?

   _____

   _____

   _____

8. Are you presently involved in legally divorcing? At what stage in the process are you?

   _____

   _____

   _____

9. Are you or your ex-spouse presently dating? How do your children feel about these other people, if any? Do these people have children from a prior marriage? How do your children feel about them?_____

   _____

   _____

   _____

10. Are there any other changes in the home situation (moving, parent working, etc.)?

    _____

    _____

    _____

CUESTIONARIO PARA PADRES

Direcciones: Responda solo a las preguntas que se sienta comodo, este cuestionario es confidencial. El lider del grupo usara las respuestas para obtener conocimiento y sensibilidad sobre la situacion de su niño. Completar esta forma es voluntario, y su niño no sera excluido del grupo si usted decide no llenar la forma.

NOMBRE DEL NIÑO _____

NOMBRE DE PADRE Ó GUARDIAN _____

NOMBRE DE PADRE NO GUARDIAN _____

1. ¿Cuando sucedió esta separación? _____
_____

2. ¿Puede usted compartir un poco sobre la razón que usted y su esposo/esposa tuvieron para decidir la separación? _____
_____
_____

3. ¿Cuando y como ha explicado usted la razón de la separación a los niños? _____
_____
_____

4. ¿Como los niños reaccionaron immediatamente y despues de la separación? _____
_____
_____

5. ¿Sus niños han hecho cosas de las cuales usted esté consciente hayan sido con el proposito de que ustedes se reconsilien? _____
_____
_____

6. ¿Cuales son las disposiciones para las visitas? ¿Cuan frecuentes, donde, por cuanto tiempo, quien recoje y quien deja los niños? ¿Están funcionando las reglas establecidas de visitas? _____
_____
_____

7. ¿Usted y su esposo todavia tienen conflictos mayores? ¿Estos conflictos son con relacion a los niños, como por ejemplo el apoyo economico de los niños y visitaciones? ¿El niño esta consciente de estos conflictos? _____
_____
_____

8. ¿En este momento se encuentra usted en el proceso legal de divorcio? ¿En cual etapa del proceso de divorcio se encuentra en este momento? _____

    _____

    _____

9. ¿Está usted o su ex-esposo actualmente saliendo con alguna persona? ¿Como se sienten sus niños con estas otras personas, si hay alguna? ¿Estas personas, tienen niños de matrimonios anteriores? _____

    _____

    _____

10. ¿Hay otros cambios en la situacion de la casa como por ejenplo mudanzas, padres trabajando, etc? _____

    _____

    _____

TEACHER NOTIFICATION FORM

Date: _____

To: _____

From: _____

The student(s) listed below will be participating in a Children of Divorce support group. The group will meet once each week on the following day, _____, at the following time, _____. The group will last for twelve weeks and will meet in the _____ office. The first session will be held on _____.

Student Names:

General Background

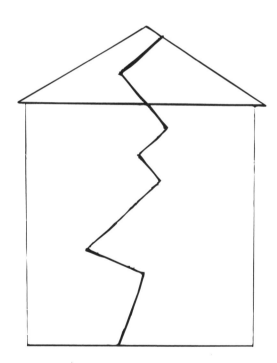

Statistics and Purpose of Divorce

In 1984, when I was a social work intern at an elementary school in Evanston, my supervisor and I did a needs assessment to determine what percentage of children in the school were living in two-parent intact families and what percentage were not. The latter category included single-parent families (parent was either never married or was separated/divorced) and remarried ones. What we discovered was that exactly 50 percent were intact and 50 percent were not.

Edward Teyber, in his book *Helping Children Cope With Divorce*, says that in the 1990s over 1.1 million couples divorce each year. In the United States, one out of two new marriages ends in divorce, most within the first ten years. Over one-third of the children will experience the divorce of their parents.

There are two primary reasons why couples choose to divorce. The first is to get out of a marriage that is not working for at least one of the partners. The second is to get another chance to build a new life.

Stages of Divorce

Judith Wallerstein describes three broad, overlapping stages of the divorce process, but not all families or individuals progress through all three. It is possible to remain stuck in one.

The first stage includes the increasing marital strife that culminates in one parent leaving the household. It continues for several months or for a year or two after the separation. It is marked by chaos and disorganization in the household. Children often witness anger and sometimes physical violence between their parents. They may become aware of a parent indulging in sexual relationships. Divorcing parents are usually preoccupied during this initial period, so daily routines deteriorate, discipline and rules are followed inconsistently. The children yearn for more attention at this time of stress, yet the distracted parents generally give them less. Parents are struggling to cope with the crisis of divorce and tend to be less sensitive to the needs of their children.

The second stage, according to Wallerstein, is a transitional one. It is when adults and children attempt to rebuild their lives in new ways. Adults may return to school, get new jobs, move to new homes, seek out new relationships. Children often move, make new friends, attend new schools. Life has not settled into stable and predictable rhythms, but attempts at rebuilding are being made.

In the third stage, the family has become fairly stable. Visitation and child support patterns have been established. Living and school arrangements are settled. New relationships have been found to replace former ones. However, this family is still more vulnerable to crisis than when it was intact. There are more financial strains, there is less support during emergencies, and there are more burdens coping with everyday life on a single-parent. And if the parent remarries, then a new period of instability occurs.

General Effects of Divorce on Children

Researchers have found that there are short- and long-term effects of divorce on children. The short-term effects tend to be similar and are discussed in this book. One reason support groups are so beneficial, is because the children have, for the most part, experienced many of the same short-term effects and can communicate these with each other. However, the long-term effects vary, depending on how the parents respond to their children and on the degree of harmony the children experience after the divorce. Children who continue to witness frequent and intense parental conflict, who are abandoned by a parent, or who suffer from constant inattention will remain at an early stage of the divorce process. They yearn for parental reconciliation rather than accept the family reality. They stay stuck instead of facing new developmental tasks necessary for growing. These children are often depressed or angry and have problems academically, socially, and behaviorally.

Many studies have been done comparing children from divorced homes with those from intact ones where parents always fight. The findings show that the former generally come out healthier psychologically and behaviorally. Children cannot prevent their parents from divorcing. But they can develop into healthy adults if their parents keep their conflicts between themselves and continue to have positive relationships with them. Parents need to spend enjoyable time with their children — conversing at dinnertime, doing chores together, going on outings, or playing games. Love flourishes at these times.

SESSION 1 *LESSON PLAN*

Aim:	1. To begin to get to know the members of the group and feel comfortable disclosing personal stories.
	2. To begin to understand that there are others who share mutual experiences and feelings about parental separation.
Materials:	1. Optional: "Sentence Completions" worksheet
	2. Optional: Cards from a board game such as the *Ungame* or *Talking, Feeling, Doing Game*
	3. "Ideas About Divorce" worksheet
	4. Pencils
Procedure:	1. Say, "Before we begin, we need to get to know each other's names." The person on the right says his/her name. The next person says his or hers and the first person's name. The third person says his/hers plus the names of the two who went before. In this way, the group proceeds around the table clockwise.
	Say, 'This time we'll do the same thing as before, but after you say your name, tell one thing you like to do in your free time."
	Proceed around the group, as above, but in a counter-clockwise direction.
	2. Say, "To get to know each other a little more, we'll go around the circle, and each person will complete a sentence." Distribute "Sentence Completions" worksheet. Go around the group several times until each person has had two or three turns. (Optional alternative is to have group members draw a card from a board game and answer the question on the card.)
	3. Tell the purpose of the group, that each person has parents who have recently separated or divorced. Say, "Separation or divorce brings many changes to a family, some good, some bad. Tell us a little about the separation/divorce in your family."
	Some suggestions are: Why did your parents get divorced? With whom do you now live? Do you get to see the parent you don't live with?). This should be open-ended so that each person shares only that with which he/she feels comfortable.
	4. Have children complete "Ideas About Divorce" pretest as leader reads the items aloud.
	Say that each person will probably answer differently because each one may feel different about the separation in the family. Say, "When we are ending the group, the same 'test' will be given to you to see if your feelings or thoughts have changed."
Closing:	Say, "Because we will all be connected to each other during these sessions, we will close today by playing the 'Knots' game to show how connected we are." See "Closings," item 1 in the Introduction.

SENTENCE COMPLETIONS

1. The age I'd most like to be is _____ because _____.

2. When I'm at home, I like to _____.

3. One toy or game I have is _____.

4. My favorite subject in school is _____.

5. If I were an animal, I'd be a _____ because _____.

6. A birthday present I'd like to receive is _____.

7. During the summer, I like to _____.

8. If I could go anywhere, I'd go to _____ because _____.

9. If I had a lot of money, I'd buy _____.

10. If I could be a famous person, I'd be _____ because _____.

11. My favorite TV show is _____.

12. My favorite movie is _____.

13. I like (don't like) my house because _____.

14. A pet I have (or would like to have) is _____.

15. The person I get along with best in my family is _____ because _____

    _____.

16. My favorite friend is _____ because _____

    _____.

17. My favorite food is _____.

18. When I'm outdoors, I like to _____

    _____.

Name _____ Date _____

IDEAS ABOUT DIVORCE
PRETEST

Check to show how you feel at this time.

	Never	Sometimes	Usually	Always
1. Divorce is a very bad experience.				
2. When people marry, they should stay married.				
3. Divorce is better than having parents argue all the time.				
4. Life stays pretty much the same for kids after the divorce as it was before the divorce.				
5. When parents get divorced, it can be the children's fault.				
6. I like visiting the parent I don't live with.				
7. I can talk about the divorce with my parents, relatives, or friends and they will listen and understand me.				
8. Parents should get married again after a divorce.				
9. Stepparents are usually mean to the children.				
10. I feel sad and angry about the divorce.				

ADAPTATIONS FOR SESSION 1

For Nonreaders and Nonwriters

1. Tell the children the names if they can't remember them.

2. Do not distribute the sentence completions. Just present them orally one at a time. Or read aloud the cards from a ready-made game.

4. Read pretest aloud in the following way: "I never, sometimes, usually, or always feel that divorce is a very bad experience."

For Older Children

4. Have these children complete the pretest silently, and allow them to share, if they wish, the one or two items about which they feel the strongest.

For Classroom Groups

1. The name game is not necessary for established classroom groups unless the leader is someone other than the teacher who needs to learn the children's names.

2. This can be done in small groups of four to six.

3. Tell the students that the purpose of the group is to learn about each other's families and about the many different kinds of families people have. Suggest they tell a little about their own families (i.e., with whom they live, what the family does together, with whom they get along best, etc.)

4. Omit the pretest.

Closing: Do the Knots game in smaller groups of six to ten.

Why Parents Marry and Divorce

Telling Children Why Parents Divorce

Children of all ages are capable, on some level, of understanding that their parents are separating and will be living apart. They need to understand, at a level that is appropriate for them, why their parents are making this decision, in order to eventually be able to work through the separation issues and come to some acceptance of the situation. Children can usually cope with the truth even though it may be painful and may stir up many feelings. Worse than hearing the truth is when they are not given an explanation for the impending separation. Then, children tend to fantasize their worst fears. And because no one has told them otherwise, they believe their fantasies are true. One such fear is that they were responsible for the breakup because of their bad behavior.

Ideally, parents should sit down with all the children in the family and explain that they are separating, when the separation will occur, why the decision was made, and what sort of visitation schedule will be set up so the children can continue to see each parent. Children's questions should be answered at this time and in the weeks that follow. If, when I speak with parents prior to the first group session, I discover that they have not fully explained to their children why they have separated, I encourage them to do so at this time. Together, we formulate a clear and truthful reason on the child's level of understanding. I also request permission to reinforce this explanation in the group.

There are times when it is clear to a child why his parents are separating. Perhaps one parent is an alcoholic. Maybe there has been constant arguing in the house because the parents can't agree on a host of issues like money, work, politics, friends, activities, raising the children. One parent may have chosen another partner to love. A parent may be violent, have excessive gambling problems, be unable to hold a job, be mentally ill, or be sexually or physically abusive to a child. In these cases, children are more apt to understand and accept the need for a separation, even if they don't like it. However, in a group, they may be reluctant to express the painful details of why their parents are no longer living together. Sometimes it helps when they hear other children being very open and verbal. The leader may need to speak with the child privately and ask if it is all right to mention facts about the family in the group.

There are times parents separate for more subtle reasons. They may have drifted apart and no longer have much in common, so the marriage feels dead, or one partner may feel an overwhelming need to "find himself" without the constraints of spouse and children. There may not have been any overt signs, like fighting, in the household, so the children are baffled and shocked when told their parents are separating. These children especially need to be told why their parents are divorcing. One explanation that they can understand is that their parents no longer love each other.

Why Parents Marry

It is helpful to tell the child that his parents did love each other at the time of the marriage—if this is true. The child, in this case, was a product of their love.

However, there are many other reasons couples marry. One partner may have felt lonely, needed money, wanted to leave home, or wanted to have a baby. If a child is interested in knowing why his/her parents married and asks, the parents should tell him/her.

Reunification Fantasies

Almost every child has reunification fantasies for several months and up to one and even two years. After the separation, most children continue to wish that their parents will get back together and that they will all be a happy family again. Even when family life has greatly improved following a separation and there is peace in the house, children still persist in hoping their previously married parents will reunite.

Children tend to deny the reality of the separation. There are several reasons for the denial. Foremost is the need to avoid the pain caused by the breakup. It is overwhelming to absorb the pain all at once, so the children cope by gradually accepting the reality over time.

Sometimes, however, there are justifiable reasons for the child's difficulty in accepting the finality of the separation or divorce. The parents themselves may not be certain of their decision to separate. Also, there are some couples who have previously broken up and then reunited. The children who witnessed this once are likely to have stronger hopes that it will happen again. Then there are the children who have heard their parents repeatedly threaten to separate, but, in their past, the threats did not come true. They may feel that this separation also will not be permanent. A difficult scenario is when a parent, who was abandoned by a spouse and who wants very much to reunite, encourages reunification fantasies in the children. All of these children must be told that the separation and divorce are final.

Some children persist in having this fantasy—even after several years, even after one or both parents have remarried. These children are prevented from coming to terms with the reality of their lives and from moving on. They remain stuck, trying to figure out what they can do to get their parents back together. Some children have learned that if they have a problem, like stealing, failing classes, or becoming ill, their separated parents may come together to help their mutual child. These children are trying to control their parents, and this can produce serious problems. The message they must hear is that the separation or divorce is final and that there is nothing they can do to alter it.

SESSION 2   LESSON PLAN

Aim:
1. To insure that each person has a realistic understanding of why his/her parents separated.
2. To learn that there are many reasons that couples marry and divorce.
3. To appreciate how most children have reunification fantasies, and to begin to accept that parental separation/divorce is, in most cases, final.

Materials:
1. "Family Album" worksheet
2. Pencils

Motivation:
Ask, "Does your family keep an album of photos?

What kind of pictures are included?

Why do you think families often create albums?"

Procedure:
1. Say, "Today we will design our own album pages to tell about our families." Distribute the "Family Album" worksheet.

2. Leader will read the caption under the first frame and children will draw a picture to illustrate. Those who wish will show and describe their pictures.

3. Leader will read caption in the second frame and children will draw a picture to illustrate.

Again, those who wish will show and describe their pictures.

4. Leader will read caption in the third frame and group members will illustrate and then show and describe their pictures if they wish.

Say, "There are many reasons why people marry. Do you know any others aside from the ones already mentioned?" (List: love, money, children, loneliness, etc.)

5. Leader will read caption in the fourth frame and children will illustrate and then voluntarily show and describe their pictures.

Some may need help understanding the actual reason for the separation. Sometimes I tell them what I have learned, or I just help them clarify their understanding by talking about it in the group. I also encourage them to speak with their parents to find answers.

6. Leader will read caption in the fifth frame and children will illustrate and then voluntarily show and describe pictures.

If the child draws a picture of his parents reuniting, ask, "Do you think this will really happen?"

Say, "Most children from divorced families, when asked what they want in the future, usually say they want their parents to get back together. Sometimes this happens, but in most cases it does not. Separation is usually final, and divorce is almost always final. Even though children don't like it, they can't do anything about it. They just have to accept it."

Closing: Say, "To make sure we all remember each other's names, let's go
                  around the circle and say 'goodbye' or 'see you soon' to each per-
                  son in the group using the person's name." Then, do "closing"
                  item 6: With his/her finger, one child will write the first letter of
                  the name of someone in the group on the back of the person next
                  to him/her. The latter will say what the letter is and then guess
                  the person's name. Go around the group until everyone has had
                  a turn "writing" and "being written on."

Name _____ Date _____

FAMILY ALBUM

A Happy Time with My Family

An Unhappy Time with My Family

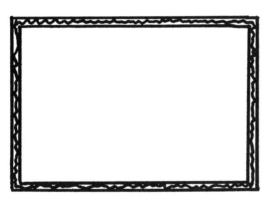

Why I Think My Parents Got
Married

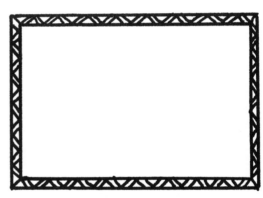

Why I Think My Parents Got
Separated/Divorced

How I Want the Future to be
in My Family

ADAPTATIONS FOR SESSION 2

For Nonreaders and Nonwriters

The activity does not need modification.

For Older Children

Many may want to use words instead of pictures. Encourage them to do both, draw and then add a caption. Many choose to add balloons and have the people in their pictures say words.

For Classroom Groups

Whenever the students are asked to share, choose just a few students who wish to do so, and tell the others you'll call on them for one of the other pictures.

5. Omit.

Closing: Omit.

• SESSION THREE •

Changes

Parental separation has a domino effect on the family system. When a couple decides to separate, the foundation of the family system is shaken, and many of the building blocks the family created together are either shaken, fall, or are recreated to form a new family system. Naturally, the children, as part of the system, are directly affected by the numerous changes that occur as a result of the parents' decision to separate.

Changing Rules and Discipline Styles

The most obvious and immediate change is that one parent is no longer living in the home. The children are now required to spend time in two different households, often sacrificing free time with friends to comply with this newly imposed schedule. The parents may each have different rules and discipline styles that can confuse the child. Children are more insecure at this time and may push limits and test boundaries to see if their parents are still in control of them.

Moving and Making Friends

Often the custodial parent moves, either to start over again or, more commonly, to a more affordable residence. Then, if the parent decides to remarry, there is often another move not long after the first one. The children must adjust to a new apartment or house; but what is more important, they have to leave their friends and make new ones. Leaving friends is another loss for them in their already fragile state. Making new friends, under the best of circumstances, can be stressful, but the child of divorce is already feeling insecure, so the task becomes even more difficult. If they appear too fragile, bully-types will sense this and be drawn to make fun of them. If they attempt to cover their insecure feelings by becoming aggressive, it will be even more difficult for them to make friends.

Even when children don't move, they may still have social problems. They may feel ashamed that their parents have separated and may not want to invite anyone to their home where this would be revealed. Children may also be experiencing a great deal of pain and feel that none of their friends care. The friends may be feeling uncomfortable because they don't know what to say or do to make their friend feel better, so they stay away for a while. Then, there are children who are experiencing intense feelings that, in the case of depression, cause them to withdraw from social contacts, or, in the case of anger, may result in their acting out toward their once close companions.

A Working Parent

Children may feel lonely for other reasons too. Just at the time when one parent has left the home, the other often must either return to work or increase working hours to compensate for the loss of income the noncustodial parent contributed to the household. In some cases, when the children are finished with school the parent is working, and the children must either stay by themselves, go to a baby-sitter, join an after-school group in a park district, or go to daycare.

Then, when the parent gets home, he or she must take care of myriad household responsibilities. Custodial parents who have just undergone a separation find tremendous demands placed upon them at a time when they are emotionally drained and less able to cope. There are responsibilities at work, in the home and garden, in finding a new emotional support network, and in caring for and disciplining the children who are especially needy. He or she is often short of time and energy and doesn't give as much of either of these as the child was used to prior to the divorce. Whereas before there were two to do the work, now there is one. Not only do the children experience the traumatic departure of one parent, but they also become aware that the other parent is harried and stressed and not very available to them. It doesn't help to tell the parent not to work, for he or she must provide for the needs of the family. The children, feeling insecure and angry at this unstable time, may take out their feelings on the parent or siblings in the home. But if the parent is stressed and emotionally out of control, he or she does not handle the situation well, and the child becomes even worse.

Money Problems

A significant drop in the income level is common for families who separate and divorce. There are many scenarios that can cause this to happen. A custodial parent may have remained at home to take care of the children and, without a work history, may have difficulty finding a job with a substantial salary. A noncustodial parent may resist providing child support. A custodial parent may have preschool-aged children in the home and must either pay for daycare with an already meager salary or go on welfare. In higher socioeconomic brackets where the financial condition is not so bleak, the lifestyle of the children may be affected nonetheless, like no money for computers, vacations, after-school lessons, summer camp, or private college.

More Responsibilities for the Children: Parentrification or Regression?

Because the custodial parent now has to assume many of the responsibilities both parents formerly shared, he or she tends to rely more on the children to help. These added responsibilities can be healthy for a child growing up. He or she can learn to become competent performing household tasks such as shopping, baby-sitting, and cleaning.

But if the child is given too many household responsibilities and is also asked to meet too many of his or her parent's emotional needs, then, in fact, he or she is being treated by the parent as a replacement for the missing partner. Either the mother or the father can use the child as an adult companion in social or recreational settings, talk to the child about very personal matters, or ask the child to advise them about adult affairs. In this role reversal, the parent becomes more dependent on the child than is the child on the parent. One problem that may show up immediately is that the child may have problems making friends with his peers because he acts too grown up. But the advantages for the child of being privy to the adult world may outweigh the problems at this point. Many children feel flattered and powerful when put in this adult role. The problems of parentrification, which is what this role reversal is called, may not be evident until the child reaches late adolescence or early adulthood. Childhood dependency needs have not been met, and so as an adult she grows to resent this deprivation. She becomes an adult who is excessively responsible for others and guilty about taking care of her own needs.

At the opposite end of the scale is the child who is encouraged to regress to earlier developmental levels. After a trauma such as parental separation, it is not uncommon for children to regress. They may start talking like babies, sucking their thumbs, soiling or wetting again, feigning illness to avoid the demands of school, having temper tantrums, or clinging. But if the regression lasts longer than a few months after the separation, the parents may be overindulging the child and encouraging the regression. A father or mother may allow some baby talk or immature behavior immediately after the separation, but tolerance should be reduced as time passes.

Academic and Behavior Problems

Teachers need to be told if and when the parents of a child in their class are separating. This knowledge will help them to understand sudden changes, either academic or behavioral, that almost always occur. Teachers may notice that a child has suddenly become more restless, is barely able to concentrate, or seems to be daydreaming for much of the school day. The child may start clinging to the teacher and be less interested in playing with peers. The child's grades may go down and assignments may be incomplete. He or she may feel inferior at this time, thinking that other kids whose parents seem happily married are better. More severe symptoms may show up if there is a great deal of distress in the home, symptoms like stealing, pervasive sadness, extreme aggression. Boys tend to become overaggressive, and girls to withdraw. By tuning in to the underlying reason for changing behavior, teachers can become allies instead of adversaries.

Improved Parental Relationships

On the positive side, strong bonds can develop between children and their parents after the separation. The children can relate exclusively to the one parent with whom they now live to talk over the day's events, play games, seek advice, go on outings, do chores together. There is no other adult in the house to interfere with this one-on-one communication. The strong bond can develop with the noncustodial parent as well. They meet together and spend time dedicated to furthering the connection between them. This visitation provides a potential time to help them develop a deeper and more intimate relationship.

For some children, the numerous changes that come with parents separating may be the challenge that enables them to attain added strength and maturity. For others, especially if the conflict between the parents does not cease after the separation, dealing with so many changes can be draining. If too much physical and emotional energy is used in coping, the child may not have enough left to deal with age-level developmental issues. The result may be delays in emotional growth. Parents should try to provide as stable an environment as possible during this transition to a new family structure. Changes are stressful. Whenever possible, parents should minimize these for their children's comfort.

SESSION 3   LESSON PLAN

Aim: 1. To understand that change is part of life, and that there are many changes that occur in a family after a separation or divorce.

                2. To appreciate that some changes are stressful, but that others improve the quality of life.

Materials: 1. "Changes" worksheets (3)

                2. Scissors and glue or tape

                3. Markers

Motivation: Say, "Everything in life changes. Let's start with a tree. How does a tree change in each season?"

Procedure: 1. Ask, "Can you think of some other things that change?"

                   "How can a family change?" (children, aging, divorce, etc.)

                2. Distribute "Changes" worksheets.

                   Say, "There are many changes that may happen in a family when parents separate or divorce. As I read each one, put an 'x' in the box in the right corner of the frame if that change occurred in your family. Leave the box blank if the change did not occur." (One blank frame is provided for a change anyone wishes to add.)

                3. Have children cut out frames marked with an "x", and glue or tape them on the blank sheet titled "Changes." Some may need to use both front and back of the sheet.

                4. Say, "Of all the changes you cut out, put a circle around the one that was the most difficult for you." Volunteers may share.

                5. Say, "Now, put a heart around the change that made things better in your family." Those who wish may share.

Changes
(caused by separation or divorce)

Having less money	Moving to another house or apartment	Being alone or with a babysitter more because parent needs to work
Having more arguments or fights with brothers and sisters	Eating either too much or too little	Having more responsibilities
Moving and having to make new friends	Having to live in two different places	Having to follow new rules

RULES
1.
2.
3.

Changes

(caused by separation or divorce), continued

Moving and having to change schools

Having a parent date or fall in love with someone else

Seeing a family counselor

Not having as much arguing and fighting in the house

Getting poorer grades in school

Spending less time with one or both parents

Having more arguments or fights with friends or classmates

Spending more time with a parent

Report Card

CHANGES

ADAPTATIONS FOR SESSION 3

For Nonreaders and Nonwriters

The activity does not need modification.

For Older Children

1. Some children, when asked, "Can you think of some other things that change?" immediately talk about family changes. Compliment them for guessing your next question and ask the group to continue to think of other things in life that change. Then say, "_____ mentioned that families change by divorcing. Can you think of any other ways a family can change?"

3. While they are cutting and pasting their pictures, ask them to talk about some of the changes they selected: Describe the change, when it occurred, how it was for them and other members of the family, how it is now, etc. The discussion should not be too structured.

For Classroom Groups

2. Say, "There are many changes that may happen in a family. As I read each one . . ."

Two Houses

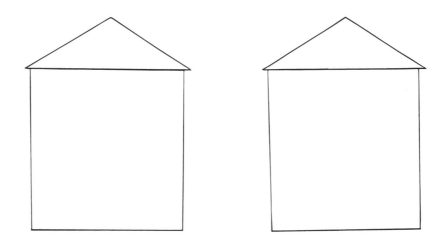

Child Exposure to Parental Conflict

Conflict often continues between the parents following the separation. There are still many issues to resolve, including custody and visitation. Often, children are exposed to these conflicts and suffer greatly. Research has shown that parent battling that is audible and visible to the children is a primary cause of their poor adjustment in school, with peers, and toward adults. They become fearful that harm will come to either one of their parents or to themselves. They do not feel secure in this battle zone. In addition, the parents are often more stressed and have less energy for parenting them. If even one parent attempts to refrain from battling, this helps the children to feel there is an island of peace, safety, and security.

Child Entanglement in Parental Conflict

Some parents go even further than just warring between themselves and get their children involved in their marital struggles. One way they do this is to criticize the other parent to the children. It is best for the children to remain detached and not take this criticism too seriously. The child needs to understand that the criticizing parent is angry and that is why he or she is saying these things. Has the child ever witnessed this behavior in the other parent and is it really accurate? And if it is, the child needs to realize that no one is perfect and that he or she will feel best loving both parents.

Loyalty Conflicts

Sometimes a parent wants the comfort of knowing he or she is close to the children at the time the marriage is breaking apart. This father or mother may feel jealous and betrayed if the children show equal interest in both parents. He or she may want the children to think he or she is the good one and the other parent is bad. The father or mother wants the children to side with him or her. These feelings are understandable, but if they are acted upon and the children are pressured to choose a side, the more poorly adjusted to the divorce the children will be. Instead, children need to be reassured that it is best to love both parents. If a parent forces a loyalty conflict, the children should be advised to tell the parent that they do not wish to take sides and that they love both parents. When parents separate, the best gift they can give to their children is the message that it is okay to love and be close to both parents equally.

The Child in the Middle

In the period following a separation, some parents no longer speak to each other and try to use the children as messengers. They say, "Please tell your mother _____," or, "Tell your father that I said _____." The children need to tell the parents that this role is upsetting them and that they should speak to each other directly.

Sometimes a parent uses the children as spies to find out what the other parent is doing. For example, he or she may ask, "Is your mother dating anyone?" or, "How much money did your father spend on that?" The children may answer to please, but feel uncomfortable being used in this way. They can state that they don't like being questioned and that the parents should question and respond to each other and not use them as go-betweens.

There are also times when children can put themselves in the middle unbeknownst to the parents. They may try to ally themselves with one parent by saying actual or imagined negative things about the other parent, or they may tell one parent that the other never gives them certain things in order to get what they want. Of course, if there is communication between the parents, the children's manipulation is discovered and can be stopped.

Being Used as a Weapon

Another way children can be put into the center of parental conflict is when a mother or father uses them as weapons of revenge. For example, a custodial parent may not allow the children to visit the noncustodial parent, or the noncustodial parent may not send child support payments. The children suffer the most when these revenge tactics occur, but have little power to effect change. All they can do is tell the parent acting out the revenge how it feels and affects them.

Spoiled Children

Once a visitation schedule has been established, new problems may arise. Often, children spend the weekdays with one parent and every weekend or alternate weekends with the other. They may also live with one parent most of the year and visit the other, who usually lives out of state, for long holidays and during the summer. It frequently happens that the noncustodial parent feels bad about leaving the children and overcompensates when they come to visit by spoiling them. He or she may become excessively indulgent by giving them any toy or food treat they want and by taking them out for amusement every day. Or the parent may become too permissive by exercising no control or discipline. Either can be detrimental to the children in many ways. Children really want a parent to love and care for them like sons and daughters, not princes and princesses. A certain amount of time spent going to places like the zoo or movies is fun. But if most of the visitation time is spent in this way, children miss doing the little everyday things that are more important when growing up, like staying home together, getting help with homework or a project, eating meals together, working together, and talking. Children who get toys too easily soon realize that that isn't what they really wanted. They get tired of the toys quickly and lose pleasure in things. When the children are not disciplined, they do not learn correct behavior and may have problems in other settings where certain behaviors are expected and others not permitted. Also, children may grow resentful of the custodial parent who must make sure the children do the everyday things like going to school, going to bed on time, and doing homework. When one parent overindulges, the children may look upon the second parent as a despot.

Parental Abandonment

A father or mother may abandon the children for any number of reasons. Some feel it is best to make a clean break with the family and start a new life. Others are uncertain and insecure about their role as parents and may feel too emotionally immature to function adequately as fathers or mothers. Then there are those who are very depressed after the divorce; they may either sink into a lethargy of inaction or make certain that they have no reminders of their former lives (like visits from the children) that would intensify their sense of loss and depression. Still others are deeply wounded people, usually because of childhood trauma that has not been dealt with, and, therefore, are not able to function as responsible parents.

There are also those parents who somewhat reject the children. This is more common after a divorce than outright abandonment. In this case, there is a slow erosion of the relationship with the children. The noncustodial parent may not keep promises, may visit erratically, may not call, or may show up late repeatedly. These unpredictable interactions take their toll on the child, who becomes increasingly distressed and feels rejected over and over again.

For whatever the reason, the children who feel rejected suffer greatly. Research studies have repeatedly shown that children who are abandoned do not do as well academically or socially as children of divorce whose parents remain physically and emotionally available. The children whose parents have left often feel angry. They may see themselves as being unlovable and deserving of rejection.

When a parent is rejecting or disappointing, it must be repeatedly communicated to the children that it is not because they are unlovable but rather that there is a shortcoming or serious flaw in the adult's ability to be a parent and to give love. In many cases, the absent parent still loves the child and has left the house for his own internal reasons. But when it is clear that the parent no longer cares, it is best for the children to be told the truth and to gradually learn to recognize that the parent is emotionally limited and is to be pitied, and that there is nothing wrong with the child.

The best remedy for children who have been abandoned is to find a same-sex substitute for the absent parent. A long-term relationship with a surrogate parent like an uncle or aunt, grandfather or grandmother, minister, or family friend helps the children to regain the sense that they are lovable. Organizations like Big Brothers/Big Sisters provide people willing to adopt a surrogate role.

Some children keep wishing and hoping their father or mother will change and become a more responsible parent. Some even try different ways to win back a parent's love, like writing pleading letters. If these efforts do not help, it is really best for the children to give up their attempts, find a surrogate, and move on with life.

SESSION 4   LESSON PLAN

Aim:	1. To understand that there are many kinds of families.
	2. To gain insight into some of the stressors involved in living in two homes.
Materials:	1. Leader will make two copies of the worksheets "Pictures of Family Members" so there are two women, two men, two boys, and two girls. Then cut out the figures of family members and laminate them.
	2. Three worksheets: "People who Live in My House," "Family Members who Don't Live with Me," and "Kinds of Families"
	3. Pencils
Motivation:	Say, "There are many different kinds of families in our world. Let's see how many kinds you can think of." Show the cut-out and laminated figures of family members to the group. Have each person take a turn creating a family. (Obviously, not all cut-outs will be used in each creation.)
Procedure:	1. Say, "Today we are going to learn about the family members you live with and the ones you don't live with." Distribute first worksheet. Say, "Inside the house, draw all the people who are presently living with you in your house."
	2. Distribute second worksheet as children finish first. Say, "Inside this house, draw the parent who has moved out of your house and is living somewhere else. Then draw the people with whom that parent is living. Write in the location of that house if you know it." Some children may need more than one sheet for multiple parents.
	3. While the group members are drawing, ask any of the following questions that seem applicable:

A.   Do you like living in your house or would you rather live with your other parent? Why?

B.   Who decided on the visitation schedule? Do you think it's fair? Why?

C.   Do any of you feel you are used as a messenger between the two houses? How?

D.   Does one parent try to find out information about the other from you? How does this feel? What do you do? What could you do?

E.   Does one parent say bad or untrue things about the other parent? What do you say?

F.   Is it hard for you to adjust to one house after spending time in the other?

G.   How does your family share you on holidays?

Closing:	Distribute the worksheet "Kinds of Families." Leader will read it aloud. The group members will share their drawings and help each other identify the types of family with whom they live. More than one kind for each person may be named (example: divorced and extended).

Family Members

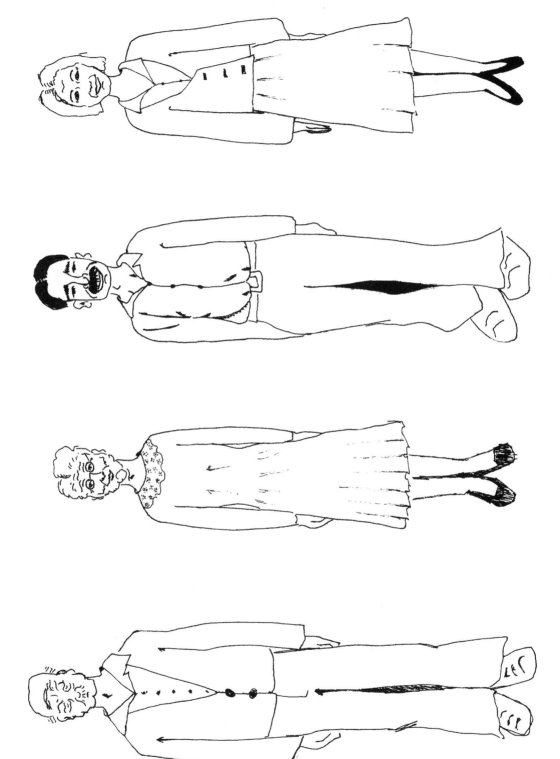

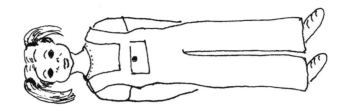

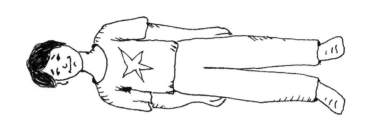

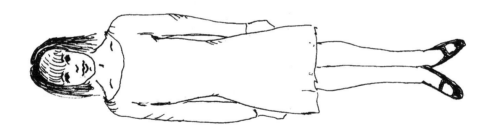

Family Members

©1996 by Sylvia Margolin

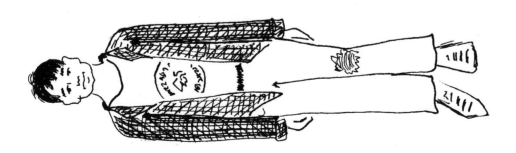

Name _____ Date _____

PEOPLE WHO LIVE IN MY HOUSE

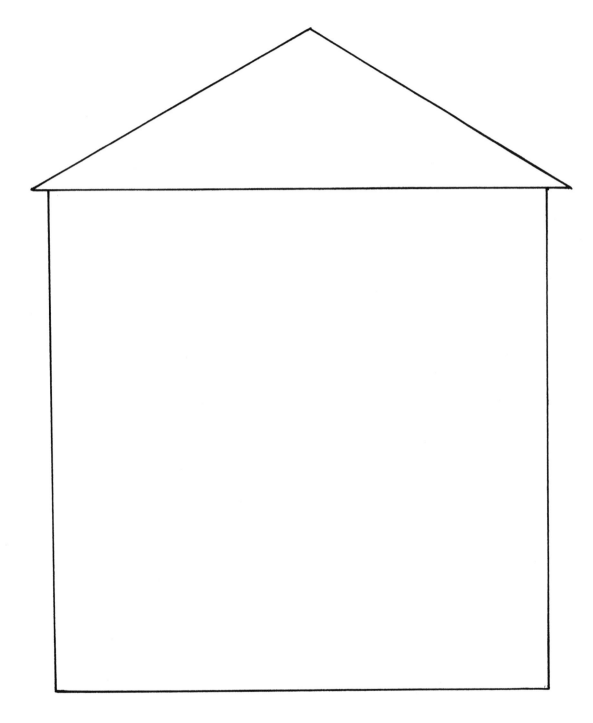

FAMILY MEMBERS WHO DON'T LIVE WITH ME

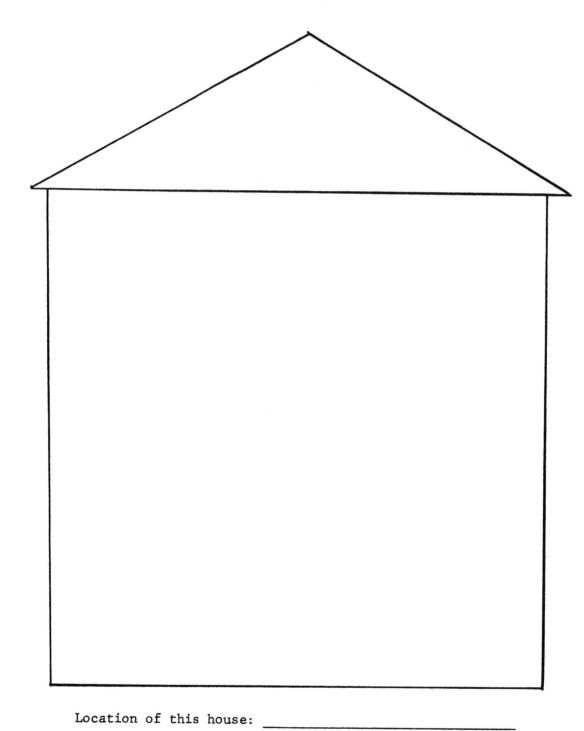

Location of this house: _____

©1996 by Sylvia Margolin

KINDS OF FAMILIES

Put a check on the line next to the kind of family in which you live. There may be more than one.

_____ 1. Traditional—father, mother, and children all live together.

_____ 2. Extended—relatives (like grandparents, aunts, uncles, or cousins) live with the family.

_____ 3. Separated—father and mother no longer live together but are not yet divorced.

_____ 4. Divorced—father and mother no longer live together, and there has been a legal end to their marriage.

_____ 5. Single-parent—children live with one parent most of the time.

_____ 6. Common-law—one parent lives with someone of the opposite sex, but they are not legally married.

_____ 7. Step—a parent married another person. The other person is called a stepparent (stepfather or stepmother).

_____ 8. Blended—a parent and a stepparent each have children from other marriages, and they all live together.

ADAPTATIONS FOR SESSION 4

For Nonreaders and Nonwriters

2. The leader should go around and write in the location of the second house if the children know it, or else, omit this part.

3. Rephrase some of the questions in simpler words.

Closing: Omit for younger children.

For Older Children

3. Ask these questions informally. The discussion should not be structured.

Closing: Older children can complete their own worksheets and then, when they show the other group members their house pictures, they can tell what kinds of families they live in.

For Classroom Groups

1 and 2. Distribute the two worksheets at the same time.

For 2, say "Inside the house on the worksheet 'Family Members Who Don't Live with Me,' draw any members of your immediate family — mother, father, brother, or sister — you don't live with. Draw them and draw the people they are living with. Then write down the location of that house or apartment. If you do not have someone in your immediate family living in another house, you can return the second worksheet."

3. Omit.

Closing: Say, "Who would like us to guess what kind of family you live with?" Show the volunteers' pictures to the class, and have people guess what kind of family this is.

• SESSION FIVE •

Feeling Angry

People get angry because they cannot get what they want. Related to anger is a sense of being powerless. Children from divorced families do not have control over the events occurring in their homes. What they want is for their parents to remain together. When their mother and father separate and then divorce, they are not getting their wishes met and, therefore, feel angry and powerless. Generally, eight- to twelve-year-old boys show anger as their predominant reaction to parental separation. However, most children of divorce have angry feelings some of the time and show them in varying ways.

Sources of Anger

There are many situations that children wish but are unable to control. They become distressed when parents constantly argue in their presence. They are angry when mom and dad separate and one parent leaves the home. If that parent abandons the family, the children may become furious. When parents are preoccupied with each other, with legal matters, or with the aftermath of separation and there is little time, energy, or affection left for the children, the latter feel hurt and angry. Sometimes a parent will take out frustrations on the children and cause them to feel resentful in return. Children get upset because their lives are in turmoil around the time of separation when parents are supposed to create secure, loving environments for them.

Internal and External Anger

Children who internalize anger instead of expressing it appropriately do so because they are either afraid of upsetting their parents, are afraid of getting punished, or feel guilty for having angry thoughts. They may use denial to hide their feelings and truly believe the anger is not there. These children tend to lose touch with their real feelings. Internalized anger may come out in the form of nightmares where the fears expressed are actually the child's rage. Repressed anger may also come out as tension like being irritable, crying easily, and overreacting to minor stress; the hidden anger is bursting to come out.

Other children externalize anger and become hostile. They act out their angry feelings in aggressive ways. Children may have temper tantrums or explosions. They may become defiant, uncooperative, or combative. They may project angry feelings for the parent who has left onto the parent with whom they live, for it is safer.

Children need to learn to differentiate between angry thoughts and feelings and angry actions. Everyone has some angry thoughts and angry feelings for we have little control over these. These thoughts and feelings are usually not hurtful to others whereas angry actions can be very destructive. Some angry outbursts are common around the time of the separation and parents need to be more tolerant than at other times. But in general, disciplinary measures must be taken for children who act out anger.

Handling Anger

When anger is expressed effectively, it can be used to help a person get the thing he or she wants, as long as that thing is obtainable. If it is not and the person can stop craving it, he or she will cease to remain frustrated and angry.

In working with children, it is helpful to teach them to become sensitive when angry thoughts and physical sensations arise. The child who denies his angry feelings won't be able to do this. A parent or counselor needs to say that the particular situation would make anyone angry, even furious, and doesn't the child have even one angry thought or a tiny angry feeling?

All children need to be encouraged to express their feelings and the cause of them as soon as possible once they are felt. For example, using an "I" statement, a child might say to a parent, "I am upset because you and mom keep arguing," or "It gets me angry, Dad, that you always come late because it seems like you don't care that much about me." This direct expression may help to change the unfavorable situation to one that is more favorable for the child, thereby causing the anger to fade.

But for most children, labeling the anger and what caused it is only the first step. The child must then do something about it, like figuring out an alternative action. For example, if parents argue, the children can go to their rooms or watch TV. If a parent is late for visitation, the son or daughter can keep busy so as not to be waiting around growing more and more resentful.

Sometimes, all attempts at expression and finding alternatives to alleviate anger do not work. The situation that is causing the anger does not change. A child could say, "It makes me feel angry that you have moved out, Dad." He or she could call, write, and plead for the parent to return to the family. But none of this brings the dad back home. When all attempts fail, children need to give up, let go of the source of the frustration, and find substitute gratification. In the case of a parent's leaving, the child can begin to find pleasure in private time spent with dad during visitation and on the phone.

SESSION 5   *LESSON PLAN*

Aim: Children often have angry feelings as a result of their parents' separation.

Materials: 1. "Role Plays" worksheet

                2. Puppets representing family members

Procedure: 1. Say, "There are many things that happen when parents get divorced or separated that can cause the children in the family to feel angry. Can you think of something that happened that made you feel angry? What did you do when you were feeling angry?"

                2. Distribute "Role Plays" worksheet. Say, "These are some of the things that happen in families who separate or divorce that cause children to feel angry. You may have already said some of these." Read the situations aloud.

                3. Say, "This time I will reread the situations, and when you find one that you want to act out, raise your hand. Or you may want to act out a family situation that is not included."

                Reread situations and give out scenes. If more than one person wants the same scene, that is okay, or else roll the die and give the scene to the one who gets the highest number.

                4. Display the puppets. Then, for each group member:

                a. Read aloud the scene he/she chose.

                b. Ask, "Which puppet characters do you need in this scene?"

                c. Ask, "Which one do you wish to be?"

                d. Ask the other group members, "Who would like to be one of the other characters in the scene? Which one?"

                e. Have child who chose scene tell the story he/she wants the group to enact. Discuss, if necessary, where the scene takes place, what the characters are doing, what is causing one of the characters to be angry.

                f. Act out the scene.

                5. Leader will select some scenes where anger led to verbal abuse or violence. Say, "It's funny when we have the puppets acting like this, but it's not funny when people in the family are abusive and violent. What could the puppet-people have done to handle their anger without hurting anyone?"

Closings: Anger scribble. See "Closings" #2.

ROLE PLAYS

1. The parent comes very late to pick the children up for a visit (or does not come at all).

2. The children overhear the parents arguing with each other.

3. The children live with one parent who is very busy taking care of the house, making dinner, and working to earn money, so there is not much time left to spend with them.

4. Because their house is too expensive since the divorce, the parent tells the children they are going to move.

5. The parents are separated. One parent starts to tell the children bad things about the other parent.

6. The children are about to visit their parent. They are told to deliver a message to the other parent: "Please tell your father/mother _____."

7. One parent starts questioning the children about the other parent. (Examples: "Is your father/mother dating anyone? Where does he/she work?")

8. It is the child's birthday. The child is reminded that his/her very own parent never remembers his/her birthday. As a matter of fact, the parent never writes, calls, or visits at all.

9. One of the child's parents has started to date someone new.

10. The child sees the parents having a bad argument, and then sees one of them slam the door and leave.

ADAPTATIONS FOR SESSION 5

For Nonreaders and Nonwriters

Younger or shyer children will often need the leader to help provide words when role playing. Leader may need to play a part to help with the dialogue.

For Older Children

The activity does not need modification.

For Classroom Groups

1. Say, "There are many things that happen in a family that may cause the children to feel angry. Can you think of one?" List these on the blackboard to use for role play instead of the suggestions on the worksheet.

• SESSION SIX •

Feeling Guilty

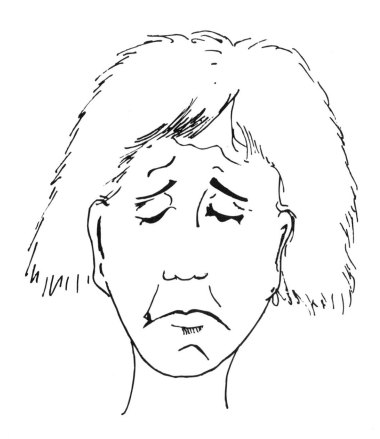

Many children blame themselves for their parents' divorce. They feel they've been bad — that they did something wrong or that they didn't do something they should have. All children do things they aren't supposed to do at times. They cannot control all their behaviors and feelings. There may be times when they break rules, fight with other children, get angry when they don't get their way. The guilty children, however, attribute the conflict and eventual separation of their parents to these misbehaviors.

Egocentric View

One reason why children, especially up to about seven years of age, may blame themselves for the divorce is because they are still egocentric in their thinking. They think that all things that happen are because of them. Because of their immature level of cognitive development, they think simplistically and do not appreciate the complex contributions the parents make to the marital problems. They need to be reassured that children are never responsible for adult decisions such as separation and divorce. They also need explanations, on a level they can understand, as to the actual cause of the separation.

Perfect Parents View

Some children blame themselves because they have the need to see their parents as perfect. If their parents are perfect, then the conflict must be about them, for they are imperfect. If the parents separate because of the conflict, it is because of them that they are separating. Some parents seem to be perfect to their children. They need to help the children see them more realistically, share with them their strengths and weaknesses in an appropriate way, explain each parent's joint contribution to the decline and breakup of the marriage.

Need to Gain Control View

Some children blame themselves for the separation because that puts the control in their hands. If they caused the conflict that led to the separation, than they can do something to bring about a reunion. These children tend to spend their energy doing things to try to get their parents together. They need to be told that they have no control over their parents' decision. They can control some things in their lives that pertain to them, but not others, like the choices their parents make. They need to stop investing time and effort in attempts to reconcile their parents and, instead, accept the reality of the separation and concentrate on developing their own lives.

Powerful Angry Thoughts and Feelings View

Young children who get angry at their parents and wish they were dead or wish that they could be replaced or wish that one or both parents could go away may feel guilty and think their angry thoughts and feelings caused the divorce to happen. If they act these out by shouting or being destructive, they are likely to feel even more guilty and terrible about themselves if the marriage breaks up. Again, they need explanations and reassurances that their thoughts and feelings show anger, but are not the reason for the separation.

When Parents Blame Children

Sometimes parents actually do blame the children for their problems. Some may not want to take responsibility for their inadequate ability to parent in a united way, so it becomes easier to shift the responsibility for the family conflicts onto the disruptive child. Others may be angry because they never wanted to have children in the first place or because the children's needs have added stress to the already meager financial situation, or because the child is born with a handicap and has become a burden to the household.

Some parents blame in an overt way. They let it be known that the child caused too much trouble and that is why they are leaving. Other parents blame in a covert way, by saying it is best for the family if they leave, that maybe with them gone there will be less trouble with the children. In either case, the children almost always develop severe and enduring problems. They need to be told again and again that children are never responsible for decisions made by their parents. The real fault lies in the inability of the parent to cope and in the parent's decision to leave.

Guilt After the Separation

Even if children do not feel guilty for causing the parental separation, they may take on these burdensome feelings afterwards. If they are asked to choose with whom they prefer to live, they may feel disloyal to one parent and thus feel guilty. Some may feel guilty because they enjoy spending time with one parent more than the other, like the "Sunday parent," who constantly entertains. Ideally, both parents should provide recreation and responsibilities. Some children may feel guilty because they do not wish to visit the noncustodial parent. In this case, they can have shorter visits or bring a friend.

Sometimes one parent in the marriage is to blame. The children have good reasons to feel angry with this parent, for his/her actions and for causing the marriage to crumble. This parent did things that were not worthy of their love and respect. In this case, the critical feelings of the children are justified and there is no cause for them to feel guilty.

Children who are preoccupied with feelings of guilt or blame are generally bogged down. They often are not tending to the tasks of growing up, like doing their school work, enjoying their friends, or engaging in productive activities. They need to let go of these preoccupations, accept that the divorce is not under their control, understand the real reasons for the breakup of the marriage, and get on with the tasks of growing and developing.

SESSION 6   *LESSON PLAN*

Aim: 1. To review the concepts already discussed.

2. To understand that it is never the fault of the child when parents choose to separate.

Materials: Book, filmstrip, or videocassette about divorce

Procedure: 1. Say, "This is a book (filmstrip) with the title _____. What do you think it will be about?" (A bibliographic list of possible books, filmstrips, and videocassettes is provided in the appendix. Choose one that deals with the issue, among others, that children are not at fault when parents choose to separate.)

2. Read book or view filmstrip or videocassette.

3. Possible discussion questions based on the story:

     a. Why do you think the parents got married?

     b. Why do you think they were getting divorced?

     c. What feelings did the boy/girl have as a result of the parents' separation or divorce?

     d. Did the boy/girl think the divorce was his/her fault? Why? Was it? Did you ever think you caused your parents to separate? Some children think this, but it's never true.

     e. What dream did the boy/girl have? What did it mean? Did you have any nightmares following your parents' separation? Tell about one.

     f. What changes occurred in the boy's/girl's life as a result of the parents' fighting, separating, or divorcing?

     g. What helped the boy/girl begin to feel better?

4. Ask, "Which part of the story do you remember most? Was it like that in your family?"

ADAPTATIONS FOR SESSION 6

For Nonreaders and Nonwriters

This activity does not need modification, but the book, video, or filmstrip used must be on the children's level.

For Older Children

This activity does not need modification.

For Classroom Groups

3c. Omit the personal question, "Did you ever think you caused your parents to separate?"

The Grieving Process

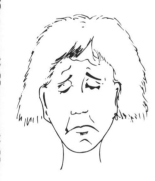  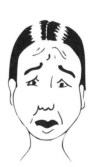 

The feelings children have when their parents break up are similar to those they feel when a parent dies. In both experiences — divorce and death — the loss of a loved one may arouse an initial feeling of shock and denial, disbelief that the loss is occurring; grief and sadness over the loss; anger directed at those responsible for allowing such a thing to happen; guilt, especially in younger children, for feeling responsible for the break up; anxiety and fear, especially of abandonment. Both death and divorce begin with a crisis and are followed by a period of readjustment that may last a year or go on for many years.

There is one major difference, however, between the two experiences. Whereas death is final and, at some point, accepted as such, divorce does not seem so to a child who continues to see both parents. These children continue to hope that the divorce can be undone at any time and that their parents will reunite. Therefore it is more difficult for them to accept the finality and move on with life. For children of divorce, the final stage in the grieving process, acceptance, is more difficult to attain. For them, feelings of hope linger on, long after the initial separation and divorce of their parents.

Shock and Denial

Children are shocked and surprised when they learn of their parents' decision to separate — even if they've known their mother and father have been arguing and have been unhappy together for a long time. Except in cases of severe abuse and neglect, children are happy to be living with both their parents in an intact family. They do not want divorce. When they witness parental fighting, they feel hopeful that it will pass, that their parents will learn to get along with each other, and that the family will become more peaceful in the future. They are feeling hopeful rather than discouraged, so when they are told of their parents' desire for separation and divorce, many do not believe it.

There are also some family situations or reactions that reinforce denial. It could be that the parents have never argued or exhibited anger in front of the kids, so children have had no preparation for the decision to separate. In this case communication about cause is essential. It could also be that there is so much happening at the time of the breakup for both adults and children, all become numb and are not able to show feelings at this time. Children may close up and not want to talk or cry. They may be confused about how they feel, or they may have so many strong feelings that they are afraid they'll burst, so they hold them in until the time is safe.

Younger children may show their denial in overt ways. They may continually ask when the absent parent is returning or pretend that the parent is away on a trip. Some children displace their concern onto another person or pet and deny having any concerns about the separation.

Anyone who works with children of divorce who are in the denial stage of the grieving process can be reassured that it is okay to remove this defense. To maintain it means that the children cannot proceed to experience more painful feelings that are inevitably there, and thereby eventually adapt to their new reality. It may be that direct discussion provokes too much anxiety, especially for younger children. Reading a story or talking about animals may be less threatening.

79

Sadness, Grief, and Depression

Typical for children following parental separation is a period of grief. They may feel very sad, cry easily, lose their appetites, experience a decreased interest in school-work and play, have trouble sleeping, and lose interest in being with their friends.

These children are grieving over the loss of their family as it once was and over the loss of the parent who has departed. Even though they do not actually lose a parent, they grieve because they may never again live with the parent who has left. Some grieve out of concern for their own welfare. How will all their needs be met by only one parent? Some grieve because they personalize the rejection. They feel that the parent is leaving them.

Usually this period of grief is short-lived. It is an expected reaction to the separation and should lift within a few weeks or months. Children who are grieving need comfort during this period. They have a great need for physical contact and reassurance. Crying is helpful because sad feelings can be released.

Some parents ignore their children's sadness. They may be absorbed in their own distress and, therefore, not be sensitive to the feelings their children are experiencing. Or they may be the type of parents who denigrate or invalidate sad feelings. They may say crying is for babies, a sign of weakness. Or they may say it is a sign of feeling sorry for yourself, brace up, other people have it worse. If these feelings of grief cannot run their course, children may try to hide them, become anxious and confused, and lose touch with their other emotions as well.

Children should have the chance to have frequent contact with the parent who has left, either by visiting or by telephone. If contact is rare, very inconsistent, or nonexistent, the reactive grief may become depression. As part of the depression, children develop a negative self-image and feel unlovable and unworthy. There must be something wrong with me, they say, or else my parent would want to be with me more. The other part of the depression is the loss of initiative, feeling helpless and hopeless, no longer feeling competent. I am a loser, they say, and I expect to fail.

As in adults, there can be an agitated form of depression. Boys, especially, may display agitated hyperactivity. They are attempting to ward off the pain of loss by escaping into movement.

Anxiety and Fear

A fear of being abandoned by parents is common in most latency-aged children. Children are dependent on adults for protection and nurturing, and, at times, fearfully imagine a life without it. Therefore, when one adult actually moves out, the security and foundation of the household is shaken. Children of divorce then often develop anxiety about being separated from the remaining parent. If one parent can go, so can the other. If there is only one parent in the home, maybe he or she will have an accident or illness, and the children will be alone. If something happens who will take care of us? These fears of abandonment are understandable given the real-life loss of the children of divorce.

The children may experience other fears as well after the separation. Will their parents fall out of love with them as they did with each other? Will each parent be able to manage without the other helping out? Will each parent be lonely without the other and will anyone love them again?

Fears and anxieties may manifest themselves in any number of regressive behaviors: bed wetting, thumb-sucking, fear of the dark, nightmares, clinging, school phobia, and somatic symptoms like head and stomachaches. These are all normal reactions to tensions and worry.

It is beneficial for these children to realize that they are frightened, and that this is a natural way to feel. They need reassurance that fears of abandonment are unwarranted. No matter what happens, there is always someone to take care of them: either parent, a relative, or a good friend. Telephoning the parent who left is important so that the child knows where the parent is and that the parent is safe. Responding to fears and anxieties with reassurance and information will help to decrease the anxiety-induced behaviors.

Confusion

Following parental separation, children may be confused about what the future will be like for them. Their known family structure has crumbled and rules, routines, and relationships may be new and confusing.

On the level of feelings, however, children may also experience confusion. Like all children, those who are going through parental separation and divorce have many feelings, but probably are feeling them more intensely at this time. There are times when these children may feel love, dislike, anger, or even hate for mother or father. Some kids may think it is wrong or bad to have mixed feelings toward a parent and need to understand that it is normal.

Sometimes these mixed feelings are felt simultaneously. Ambivalence, where two feelings are experienced at the same time, makes a child feel confused. For example, the child may love her mother but be angry with her for wanting the separation. Or the child may feel relieved that his parents are separating so the fighting will stop, but he is also angry and sad because his family is breaking up. Verbally separating the simultaneous feelings and explaining how it is possible to feel both at the same time can be very helpful.

Hope and Acceptance

Shock and denial, sadness and grief, anger, guilt, anxiety, and fear may all be part of the grieving process for those who have experienced parental death or divorce. But hope of reunion is not a rational emotion for anyone who has lost a loved one to death. Some, of course, hope to see or meet with the deceased in the next life, but nondelusional people do not hope for reunification in this life. However, children of divorce experience this hope very strongly following a separation. Regardless of age, there is an obsessive desire to have the parents get back together again. And when divorce is preceded by several separations that seem final but are not, the children have a real-life basis for this hope and desire. Only time, a clear message, and reality will cause it to diminish so that some degree of acceptance is possible. When they finally stop hoping for an impossible reunification, they can move on with life and feel better.

In some cases acceptance comes easily and early when, for example, one parent was abusive or a substance user. In other cases, children who were angry and sad in the beginning, discover, after several years, that their parents' decision to divorce has made things better for everyone. Their parents' lives are happier, there is less tension and arguing in the house, and the parents have access to more positive emotional energy for their children. Not all children of divorce can fully accept the family break-up, but those who, more or less, come to terms with this reality, are the freest to move ahead to face life's future challenges.

Developmental Stages: How Divorce Affects Children at Different Stages of Their Development

Infancy and Early Childhood. In very general terms and to somewhat run the risk of oversimplifying the complex natures of young people and their feelings, it is possible to say that different aged children have their own emotional pattern of responses to parental breakup. Even in utero, the developing fetus feels the tension and distress of the mother. The baby, when born, may be irritable, hyperactive, restless, needy, cry a lot, and have digestive or sleeping problems.

An infant under six months continues to feel the distress of the custodial parent. The infant feels this indirectly by the amount of stimulation and responsiveness he or she is given and by the quality and consistency of care.

From about eight to eighteen months, the child is forming close attachments to his or her caregivers. He or she can recognize people and will know if one of the caretakers is no longer present. From one year to eighteen months, the child experiences the direct effect of being separated from one of the people to whom he or she has become deeply attached.

From eighteen months to two years, the child is more imaginative and so has greater fears. Dreams may turn into nightmares. At this stage, children are beginning to imitate the actions of their same-sex parent. So a loss of a father to a boy or a mother to a girl is very painful.

By two, children have developed a sense of trust in their parents. They are gradually pulling away from their dependence to investigate the world around them. If parents separate at this time, the child's sense of trust is threatened. He or she may regress and become more possessive of objects, bossier, more demanding, and more fearful. The need for consistency, routine, and affection are essential at this time so the child can regain trust and renew his attempts toward independence.

Preschool. Preschool-age children begin to develop a conscience, a sense of what is right and wrong. Along with this sense of moral order comes guilt. If you do something wrong, it is bad and you feel guilty. At the same time, children of this age are egocentric and see all relationships and events as revolving around them. Therefore, if the family breaks apart, they must be at fault.

The preschool age is also the time when children develop sex-role identities by identifying with the same-sex parent and feeling romantic love for the opposite-sex parent. The inner oedipal conflict, described by Freud, begins. Children wish their same-sex parent would disappear so they could have the opposite-sex parent all to themselves. Divorce is particularly painful at this time if the same-sex parent does leave. The child feels guilty, not just for wishing the parent gone, but also because the parent actually goes. The oedipal conflict should be resolved in favor of the parent, not the child. The guilt that follows may intensify the nightmares that are somewhat normal at this stage of development. The child at age six is ready for more independence and more involvement with peers rather than more intimacy with the opposite-sex parent. Normal development may therefore be hindered.

Latency: Ages Six Through Eight. Latency can be a time when children put all their energy into becoming more independent from their families and moving closer to peers, getting more involved with learning, gaining a stronger sense of who they are. But though friends are very important, parents are still the center of the children's lives. They are role models for sexual identification and for values. They provide security and structure as the children venture out into the larger world of school and neighborhood. The loss of one parent can be devastating at this stage. Children feel that their secure world is collapsing, and they may collapse with it. A deep and pervasive sadness ensues. They cry openly and express longing for the absent parent. There is anger and fear, but above all, sadness.

Often these children feel deprived of their natural chidhood rights. They feel they are the only ones without two parents and see all intact famililes in an idealized way. They feel those kids from intact families have more money and get extra attention whereas they are deprived. Small acts of caring and attentiveness for these children help alleviate some of the anxiety they must feel about their weakened support system.

Children will stop feeling so sad and so frightened when they learn that their world hasn't collapsed as much as they thought at first. The more frequent the contact with each parent, the more confident the children will be that they are loved. Though the family structure has changed, there still is one, and their place in it is assured. The period of intense sadness will pass as the children feel more secure and as they continue to interact with the larger world of school and neighborhood around them.

Latency: Ages Nine Through Twelve. Children use their parents as guides to developing their own morality during the late-latency phase, ages nine to twelve. If they grew up in traditional families, they have learned that marriage is based on loyalty and permanence, that sex is reserved for marriage, and that there is ethical conduct in society. The moral construct, being new, is rather fragile and rigid at this time.

But when those very parents who were the role models for this moral construct no longer abide by the rules, the children become extremely angry. It is this deep anger that is the dominant emotion felt by older latency-aged children.

These children do not respond passively to parental separation. They let both parents know how angry they are, especially the one they blame for the breakup. They often make one parent all good and the other all bad. Then they will refuse to see or be defiant with the bad parent. They will be focused on getting revenge and punishing this bad parent for causing the divorce.

Girls are beginning puberty and a second oedipal phase at this time. In an intact family, the parents are united so there is not a threat that the oedipal feelings will get out of bounds. But in a single-parent home where the parent may be attempting to develop a new relationship, the atmosphere may become very sexual. Girls may compete with their mothers for new boyfriends by becoming seductive. Mothers and daughters may become competitive as both try out clothes, hairstyles, and make-up or as mothers become students once again. For both boys and girls, it becomes frightening to witness their parents become sexually active with other partners. When their peers are sexually active out of wedlock, they develop bad reputations. But their parents are engaging in the very same behaviors. They may have had affairs before the separation, they may have had sexual relationships while they were separated but before the divorce, they may have had sex while divorced but before getting remarried.

Children of this age are able to understand, to a great extent, the reasons for their parents' separation. They can see that the problems were the result of the parents' inability to get along, and they were not because of the kids' misbehavior. These children can even experience the positive results of separation, like the decrease in tension and fighting. But even so, they continue to have reunification fantasies.

The best approach to helping children of this age to deal with the family situation is to enable them to defuse their anger. It is important to stress the good points about each parent — unless one parent has been abusive or has abandoned the family. Also, children should be encouraged to participate in extracurricular activities to help them become more detached from parental problems and increase their sense of competence. Again, small acts of caring, like going out to dinner or to a movie, are very healing in relationships. In time, as the family routines become stable again, the anger will dissipate.

SESSION 7 LESSON PLAN

Aim: 1. To understand that there are many emotions that one may feel when grieving.

2. To learn that there are stages in a grieving process.

Materials: 1. 2 worksheets: "Stages of Grief" and "Feelings in the Grieving Process"

2. Pencils and either crayons or markers

Procedure: 1. Say, "Usually the first feelings children have are shock and denial when they first find out their parents are going to separate. They don't really believe that this will happen or that it will be forever. Do you remember when you first learned that your parents were getting separated? Where were you? How did you find out? Do you remember how you felt at the time?"

2. Distribute the worksheets on the grieving process. Call the children's attention to the "Stages of Grief" chart. Say, "After parents separate, children have many feelings, like sadness, anger, confusion, worry, guilt, or hope. Finally, after time passes, kids more or less accept what has happened. They might not like it, but that's how it is, and it's time to get on with life. At what stage do you think you are in the grieving process? Why?"

3. Call the children's attention to the "Feelings in the Grieving Process" color-coded chart. Read the list aloud. Then look at the first example on the first worksheet.

Say, "The boy in the example has chosen to express his feelings using circles of different sizes, each colored to represent a different feeling. What feeling does this boy have the most?" (biggest circle) "the least? What are the other feelings this boy experiences?" (Repeat, using example for the girl who expressed her feelings using triangles.)

4. Say, "Choose any shape you like and vary the size to show which feelings you have felt most or least as a result of your parents' separation or divorce. Then color in the shapes to correspond with the feelings listed on the worksheet."

5. Volunteers may show pictures. Ask the other group members, "Which feeling does _____ have the most? The least?"

STAGES OF GRIEF

| SHOCK & DENIAL | | SADNESS | ANGER | GUILT & BLAME | WORRY & FEAR | CONFUSION | HOPE | | ACCEPTANCE |

BEGINNING STAGE

MIDDLE STAGE

FINAL STAGE

BOY:

RED   BLUE   PURPLE   YELLOW

GIRL:

MIXED   BLUE   RED

EXAMPLES

©1996 by Sylvia Margolin

86

FEELINGS IN THE GRIEVING PROCESS

Shock & denial	=	brown	Worry & fear	=	orange
Anger	=	red	Confusion	=	mixed colors
Sadness	=	blue	Hope	=	purple
Guilt & blame	=	green	Acceptance	=	yellow

ADAPTATIONS FOR SESSION 7

For Nonreaders and Nonwriters

2 and 3. Repeat the words in the diagrams as needed.

4 and 5. Help the children by rereading words from the diagram.

For Older Children

4. Have the older children write under their colored shapes what makes them feel this way for the most part.

For Classroom Groups

1 and 2. Omit.

3. Start by saying, "Children have many feelings as they live in their families." Distribute worksheets and name some of these feelings that are listed. Continue #3 as is.

4. This can stay the same, but instead of saying, "As a result of your parents' separation or divorce," say, "As a member of your family."

5. Have only some volunteers share their work.

Legal Issues

Mediation

Divorce mediation is a way for couples to settle the conflicts that arise as a result of divorcing, for example, custody, visitation, and child support. The mediator remains neutral and attempts to help the two parties come to decisions. He or she does not take sides or make the decisions, but rather helps the couple to come up with imaginative solutions that are in the best interests of the family. Mediation is often likely to produce agreements that both sides feel are fair.

However mediation can also fail, especially in more extreme situations like when one or both partners have been violent or have excessively misused drugs or alcohol. When attempts to mediate fail, custody disputes go to court. It can take as long as two years for these cases to be decided. During this period, the children and parents are in limbo, uncertain about the future. Children who are asked to testify in court for one parent against the other suffer deeply. Mediation is preferable to having opposing lawyers trying to win battles for their clients. Litigious parents who are continuously battling over custody, child support, etc., have the most troubled children.

Custody

Custody is the assumption of responsibility for the daily decisions related to the health, education, and welfare of the children. Custody decisions are generally based on which parent will better serve their children's best interests. Though mothers get legal custody 90 percent of the time, fathers often don't fight for it. When they do, they win 63 percent of the time. Regardless of which parent has primary legal custody, the major determinant for the adjustment of the children is the parent's ability to be affectionate, to set and enforce clear and reasonable rules, and to communicate with the children.

There are a number of custody decisions handed down by the courts:

1. Joint legal custody - children live with one parent most of the time, but both parents share the responsibility for making important decisions for them.

2. Sole custody - all legal rights and decision-making go to the custodial parent, and visitation is granted to the noncustodial parent. This and joint legal custody are the two decisions awarded most frequently by the courts. Sole custody is usually given to the parent who is more effective and who does not bar access to the other parent.

3. Joint physical custody - parents live near enough to each other so that the children can live half the time with each parent. Children can go to the same school and be with the same friends. One arrangement is for each parent to get the children for half the week. Another may be to alternate weeks or months. In these arrangements the children benefit by having contact and involvement with both parents equally. However, it may be difficult as well because of the constant separation and reattachment. Also, joint physical custody requires a great deal of cooperation and contact between the parents, and few are capable of this degree of mutuality.

4. Divided or alternating custody - each parent has full jurisdiction over the children during his/her time with them. For example, if a parent lives out of state and the children visit during summer and long school vacations, that parent has legal custody for only those periods.

5. Split custody - one parent gets one or more children and the other parent gets the other(s). Courts don't often choose this because it means that not only do the children undergo separation from the parents, they must also endure separation from siblings.

Research has shown that about one-third of the couples who divorce cooperate in the interests of their children. They make plans for the children, discuss their problems, and attempt to provide and enforce similar rules. Another one-third of the couples are disengaged from each other but not combative. They don't coordinate activities or rules between households, yet they manage visitation without conflict. The last one-third are in continuous conflict with each other and over the legal arrangements for the children. They argue in front of the children, threaten to take the kids away, undermine each other, and seek repeated litigation.

Visitation

A regular visitation schedule that sets the specific time the children will be with each parent is essential. Schedules enable the children to feel secure that they will see the non-custodial parent at regular intervals. They minimize conflicts between the parents because neither needs to check with the other each time a visit with the children is desired. Of course, as with any schedule, there must be some flexibility to allow for change.

In most cases of divorce, mothers receive physical custody and fathers get visitation rights — usually every other weekend. Though it becomes more difficult for fathers to remain as active in their parenting role as they once were, it is best for the children when they continue their involvement.

Sometimes children resist visiting, especially when they become adolescents and want to be with their friends. It is best for these children to be permitted to choose whether or not they wish to visit at a particular time and to let the noncustodial parent know their plans in advance. Sometimes shorter visits are preferable. Sometimes they may wish to bring a friend with them.

Child Support

The courts generally award no more than one-third of a parent's annual income for child support. This is needed so that the children are not punished and deprived just because their parents are divorcing. Costs for raising them ideally should continue to be shared by both parents.

If the noncustodial parent does not fulfill his/her financial responsibilities, courts can order the garnishing of part of that parent's salary. The custodial parent does not need to hide from the children the fact that a parent is not contributing child support. It should be honestly presented to them. Visitation should not be denied as a tactic to obtain payments; this puts children in the middle of the parental conflict and denies them their relationship with either mother or father. The parent should seek to resolve the conflict by first discussing the issue with the other parent, and, if that doesn't work, getting help from a mediator or going back to court.

SESSION 8   LESSON PLAN

Aim:

1. To learn some legal words associated with divorce.

2. To gain some understanding about how the legal process works with regard to divorce.

Materials:

1. 2 worksheets: "Some Legal Words" and "Getting a Divorce"

2. Pencils

3. "Judge" robe or puppet (graduation gown can be used). Gavel can be used for effect.

Motivation:

Ask, "Have your parents been to court yet and are they in the middle of the legal process of divorcing? Have you spoken or will you be speaking to a counselor at the court?"

Procedure:

1. Distribute worksheet "Some Legal Words." Do this together. Leader will read the words, and then one definition at a time. Ask, "Who knows which word fits this definition? Fit it into the blanks of the crossword puzzle." Repeat for all the definitions until crossword is completed.

2. Ask, "Who can use one of the words in a sentence that tells something about your own family?"

3. Tell the children they will soon be appearing before the judge (leader) with a divorce case. They will be in pairs. One will role play the husband, the other the wife. They will be asked questions by the judge about what they want.

   Distribute worksheet "Getting a Divorce." The children will be divided in pairs and given time to work out their views and differences on the worksheet. Leader will go to each pair and help.

4. Partners will present their cases before the judge. Judge will ask them pertinent questions based on their worksheet responses before deciding on verdicts. (i.e., Do you have any children? Do you want custody of them? Do you live near each other? Do you work?)

Name _____ Date _____

SOME LEGAL WORDS

Divorce   Visitation

Alimony   Custody

Child Support   Joint Custody

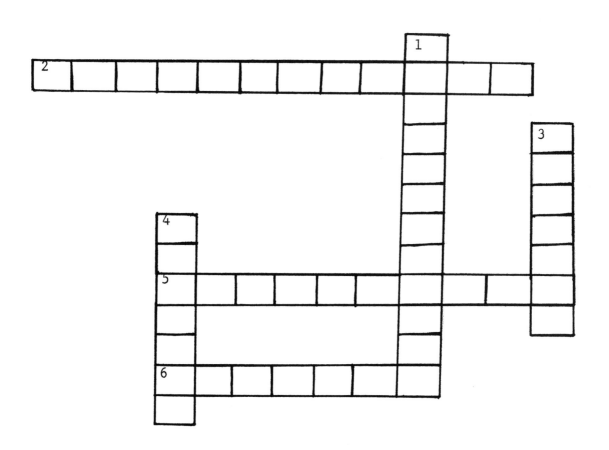

©1996 by Sylvia Margolin

Across

2. The money one parent gives the other to take care of the children.

5. The time the child spends with the parent with whom he/she does <u>not</u> live.

6. When a parent or guardian has responsibility for taking care of the children.

Down

1. When both parents share the job of raising the children.

3. The money a husband or wife pays the other to help them, after a divorce.

4. The legal ending of a marriage.

Name _____ Date _____

GETTING A DIVORCE

1. Why do you want a divorce? _____

   _____

   _____

   _____

2. Do you have children? _____ If yes, how many? _____ Do you want custody of

   them? _____

3. Do you live very near to each other at this time? _____

4. Are you working at this time? _____ If yes, do you work full-time or part-time? ___

   _____

ADAPTATIONS FOR SESSION 8

For Nonreaders and Nonwriters

1. Leader will point to the word so children can copy it into the crossword puzzle. Leader can write it in for any children who are not able to copy letters.

2. Say, "Who can use the word _____ in a sentence that tells something about your own family?" Repeat the definition in simple words as needed.

3. Leader will go around and help each pair by asking the questions from the worksheet and filling in the answers. If the group members are impatient, then do this exercise all together, asking one question at a time, having the pairs decide on their answers, and then writing them in for them.

4. The children may need help remembering or reading what their answers were.

For Older Children

This activity does not need modification.

For Classroom Groups

Motivation: Ask, "Do you know any couple who has gotten divorced? With whom do the children live?"

2. Ask, "Who can use one of the words in a sentence?"

Stepparenting

Statistically, approximately half of divorced adults remarry within one year. Seventy-five percent of women and eighty percent of men remarry within three years. The divorces are generally because people feel they are married to the wrong person, not because they are opposed to the institution of marriage. Most divorced people want to remarry. Unfortunately, sixty percent of those remarriages also end in divorce. Twenty-five percent of all children spend some part of their lives living in a stepfamily.

Fairy tales paint a grim picture of stepparents. The stepmothers in Cinderella, Snow White, and Hansel and Gretel are selfish and cruel. Some stepparents, like some natural parents, can be verbally, physically, or sexually abusive. Most stepparents, of course, are not. They have their imperfections, they may not be as understanding and affectionate as the natural parent, they may get impatient more quickly. Yet they are usually reasonable and caring adults who want the marriage to work.

Stepfamilies may look like biological families, but are actually very different. Now there may be four parents instead of two, eight grandparents instead of four, and double the number of aunts, uncles, and cousins. If the parent remarries for a second time, the number of relatives in the extended family can grow to one hundred. The two families bring different past histories, memories, customs, and habits into the marriage. They need to sort out many issues, like what name to use, where to live, whose furniture to include in the house, which rules to follow, child issues like visitation, adoption, and custody, money allocation, spouse rivalry, sibling rivalry, alimony, court disputes, loyalty conflicts. It takes between three and six years for these families to fully adjust to remarriage.

Issues for the Children

For adults, remarriage holds out the hope for a second chance at love, for a new and better home life for the family, for a partner to share the financial burdens and chores. Some children, too, very much want their parents to remarry. They may want to live in a two-parent family again. They may wish for their parent to be happier and less lonely. These children may try to bond with each person the parent dates and then feel disappointed when the relationship does not work out.

Most children, however, are opposed to and fear the remarriage of either parent. One concern they may have is that if they accept and feel affectionate for a stepparent, it is being disloyal to their natural parent of the same sex. Moreover, this natural parent might get angry with them and love them less if they accept this stepparent replacement. When these issues of loyalty arise, the children most often choose to remain loyal to the natural parent and sacrifice a warm and caring relationship with a stepparent.

Another issue with which children may deal when a parent remarries is that it hammers a powerful, if not final, blow to their reunification fantasies. Their original family is even farther apart and the hope for bringing the members closer is even less probable. Anger may flare up and be directed at the new adult in the house. These children should not be allowed to victimize the stepparent. The remarried couple must stand together to insure that the new family does not break down along blood lines.

Children may fear that if a parent remarries, he or she will not pay as much attention to them as to the new spouse. They certainly will no longer have the exclusive relationship to a single parent they enjoyed prior to the remarriage. The children have already gone through one loss, and now they fear losing the remaining parent to the stepparent. They may become angry, jealous, and disrespectful.

The children may have a deep mistrust of the new spouse. After all, their original parent left the home, so this one may leave as well. Some children remain aloof to shield themselves from a second disappointment.

Remarriage also means more change. Not only did the children of divorce experience marital break up, living in a single-parent home, possibly moving, having financial difficulties, going back and forth between two houses, parental dating, now they must adjust to becoming part of a new stepfamily. New things can be exciting, but also frightening. Often the remarriage involves yet another change of residence. The children don't know what kind of person this stepparent is, and they may think the worst. The children need to get used to the strangeness of a new person in the house and uncertainty about how this will effect their future.

Financial issues may arise. If the noncustodial parent remarries, the stepparent may resent the amount of child support given to the former spouse's family. The non custodial parent may spend more and give more to the children in the new marriage than to those in the former. If the custodial parent remarries, the noncustodial parent may resent sending child support for fear that it is being used to support the new marriage. Old problems, like child support, custody, and visitation, that were resolved at the time of the divorce, may get reopened.

Discipline Issues

Young children up to about age eight are much better able to adapt to and accept the presence of a stepparent as a member of the family. The natural and stepparent are usually able to set up a family life that is similar to the one established by the biological family. Both parents assume the nurturing and disciplinary roles. The stepparent does not replace the natural parent, but can step into the roles that parent had in the family.

However, older children, aged nine and up, consider it a problem when the stepparent tries to assume the traditional parent role. If the stepparent attempts to discipline the children too soon and before a trusting relationship is established, the children will constantly complain about how unfairly they are being treated. They will tend to set up power and control struggles rather than accept discipline. The children may see the stepparent's attempt to discipline as the latter's way of trying to replace the natural parent.

Power struggles and control battles can be avoided if the stepparent assumes the role of friend and not disciplinary parent. Relationships between stepparents and stepchildren need time to develop. The authority of the stepparent grows along with a caring and personal relationship. Stepparents need to be patient and understand the slow process that has the potential to result in the children trusting, accepting, and feeling affectionate toward them. The children should not feel pressured by the natural parent to love the new stepparent. They should be free to develop their own relationship. In time, some stepparents can assume the disciplinary role. But even if they do not, they can be an important influence in the lives of their stepchildren through their relationship as friends.

Step and Half Siblings

In the beginning, remarriage is apt to cause confusion and stress in the new household. The addition of step siblings intensifies the chaos. The children are no longer sure of their place. The birth order may suddenly be entirely different. There are many more personalities to understand and deal with. There may be rivalry for parental attention. Children may take sides along blood lines. There is more competition for getting individual needs met, like arguments about who sleeps in which bedroom. Differences in past backgrounds and expectations, like how one is expected to behave at the dinner table may cause conflict.

If the remarried couple has a natural child, the stepchildren are threatened. Will the stepparent love them as much as the biological child? There is also the potential for sibling rivalry around the issue of being natural or step children.

There will always be some children of divorce who continue to be angry and jealous and take this out on step siblings. However, if the remarried parents treat all the children equally and have warm, supportive relationships with them, and if a consistent and positive relationship with the non custodial parent continues as it was before the remarriage, then many conflicts between the step siblings smooth out in time.

Names

Younger children generally want to have the same last name as the family with whom they are living. It is less confusing for them, and it helps them to feel more connected to the family. Unless they are adopted, however, their original names are their legal names. Therefore, some families accommodate the children's feeling for union by changing the name unofficially. There are many children in school who are described by a legal name on official records, but are known by the stepfamily name among teachers and classmates.

Older children usually want to keep their original names. It may be one way to show their loyalty to the noncustodial parent, or it may be a symbolic way of holding on to what they feel is their true family, or it may just be more practical to keep the same name by which they have always been known.

Younger children are apt to begin calling the stepparent "Mom" or "Dad" shortly after the remarriage. Older children prefer to call their stepparents by their first names, rather than "Mom" or "Dad."

It usually takes from three to six years for the remarriage to become stable and for the family members to adjust to and accept it. If it works, it can benefit and enhance the lives of the adults and the children who are part of it. The children have an extra parent who cares about them, the natural parent has a new partner on whom to rely and with whom to share conversation, fun, and responsibilities, and the family is a stronger entity for the children growing up.

SESSION 9   LESSON PLAN

Aim:	To discuss feelings group members have about stepparents
Materials:	1. Book or filmstrip about stepfamilies
	2. "Feelings About Having a Stepparent" worksheet
	3. Pencils
Motivation:	Ask, "Has your mom or dad started to date yet? How do you feel about this? Do you want your mom or dad to marry someone new? Why?" Or "For those who have or are soon to have a stepparent, was it hard for you to accept your parent's remarrying? Why? How do you feel about your stepparent now?"
Procedure:	1. Ask, "Who can think of a fairy tale that has a stepparent as one of the characters?" (Cinderella, Hansel and Gretel, Snow White) "What was he/she like? What did he/she do?" "Do you think these fairy tales are fair to stepparents? Are stepparents really like this?"
	2. Say, "Even though most stepparents are not like the ones in the fairy tales, kids still may have many different feelings about their parents' dating or remarrying. We are going to read a book (or watch a filmstrip or videocassette) about having a stepparent." (A list of possible titles is included in the appendix.)
	3. "Which part of the book/filmstrip do you remember most?" Is this in any way similar to what is happening in your life?
	4. Distribute worksheet, "Feelings About Having a Stepparent." Leader will read each item and ask, "Did the boy/girl from the book/filmstrip have this feeling? When?"
	5. Have group members look over the worksheet for themselves, putting a check next to any item they either feel or think they will feel.

Name _____ Date _____

FEELINGS ABOUT HAVING A STEPPARENT

_____ 1. I am jealous of the time my parent spends with his/her new companion.

_____ 2. I feel angry because my stepparent keeps telling me what to do as if he/she were my parent.

_____ 3. I am sad that my stepparent doesn't seem to like me as much as she/he does her/his own children.

_____ 4. I worry that this marriage might end too.

_____ 5. I am happy because my parent is happy and my stepparent is nice.

_____ 6. I feel angry because I have to follow different rules and discipline in this new family.

_____ 7. I wish that this marriage would end and that my mother and father would get back together.

_____ 8. I feel happy to be in a family with two parents again.

ADAPTATIONS FOR SESSION 9

For Nonreaders and Nonwriters

4. Select a book, video, or filmstrip at an appropriate comprehension level.

7. Children can check those items they feel as leader reads the items aloud.

For Older Children

This activity does not need modification.

For Classroom Groups

Motivation: Omit.

7. Omit.

• SESSION TEN •

A *Happy Marriage*

An Adult Study

Judith Wallerstein and Sandra Blakeslee, in their book, *The Good Marriage*, describe their pilot study of fifty couples, each married for at least nine years. All the couples in the study, in the view of both partners, had achieved happy marriages.

The couples spoke about being friends. Many could not define love, but said "how much they valued, respected, and enjoyed the other person and how appreciative they were of the other's responsiveness to their needs." (p.12) All fifty couples reported not being happy at all times, that there were good times and bad times. But at the core of these good marriages was "a fit of the partners' needs and wishes." (pp. 19–20)

The authors propose that these good marriages are built upon the successful carrying out of nine psychological tasks, tasks that partners in all marriages must address:

1. Separating emotionally from the family of origin so that a new family can be created

2. Building an intimate togetherness while, at the same time, enabling each partner to remain autonomous

3. Becoming parents while still maintaining privacy

4. Coping with the inevitable crises in life while preserving the marital bond

5. Creating a safe place to express conflict — differences and anger

6. Continuing to explore sexual love and intimacy even when both partners work and become parents

7. Sharing laughter and keeping interests and social relationships alive to avoid boredom

8. Providing emotional nurturing to the partner when it is needed

9. Keeping alive the early image of love through the course of the ups and downs of a lifetime

From the Child's Vantage Point

Children whose parents did not have a successful marriage need to be reminded that it is possible for two people to live happily together. Furthermore, there are people around them — neighbors, relatives, parents of friends — who have achieved some degree of marital fulfillment.

When there is a great deal of conflict in the home, children often think that if a couple is not fighting, they must have a good marriage. It is possible to help them stretch their conception of the components of a good marriage without becoming too abstract:

1. Showing affection for one another physically (holding hands, hugging, etc.) or verbally (using an affectionate name or giving a compliment).

2. Doing things together that are fun. Though a husband or wife may have an interest the other doesn't share, it is important that there be some interests and activities both partners enjoy sharing and doing together. Some of these, like going to the movies or a restaurant or playing a sport or game, can include the children.

3. Sharing the domestic responsibilities, including household chores, child rearing, and earning money. Couples have their own ways of dividing these tasks so that both partners are participating equally.

4. Making each other laugh. Being lighthearted in a marriage makes everyone in the family feel happy.

5. Comforting each other when one partner is not feeling well emotionally or physically.

6. Being able to talk about differences and about what gets each other angry without becoming negating, violent, or abusive.

7. Helping each other when there is a crisis in the immediate or extended family, such as illness, death, financial problems, or child-rearing stresses.

SESSION 10 LESSON PLAN

Aim: To discuss what makes a happy marriage.

Materials:
1. Marking pen and paper or chalk and blackboard
2. Pictures of happy couples (7)
3. "Happy Couple" worksheet
4. Markers or crayons or colored pencils

Motivation: Ask, "Do you think you'd like to get married someday? Why or why not?"

Procedure:
1. Ask, "Do you know any couples who have a happy marriage? How can you tell?" Make a list to refer to later, using children's ideas and words (example below).

   List

   A. They hold hands, hug, or kiss.

   B. They do things and go places together.

   C. They comfort and help each other.

   D. They share the work.

   E. They talk about what bothers them.

   F. They smile and make each other laugh.

   G. They say nice things to each other.

2. Show seven pictures of couples. Ask, "What is happening in these pictures that makes us feel that the couples are happy?" Add new comments to the list.

3. Distribute "A Happy Couple" worksheet. Say, "Now it is your turn to draw a picture of the couple you know who is happily married. You can use an idea from the list we made to show them getting along well with each other."

4. Those who wish may share.

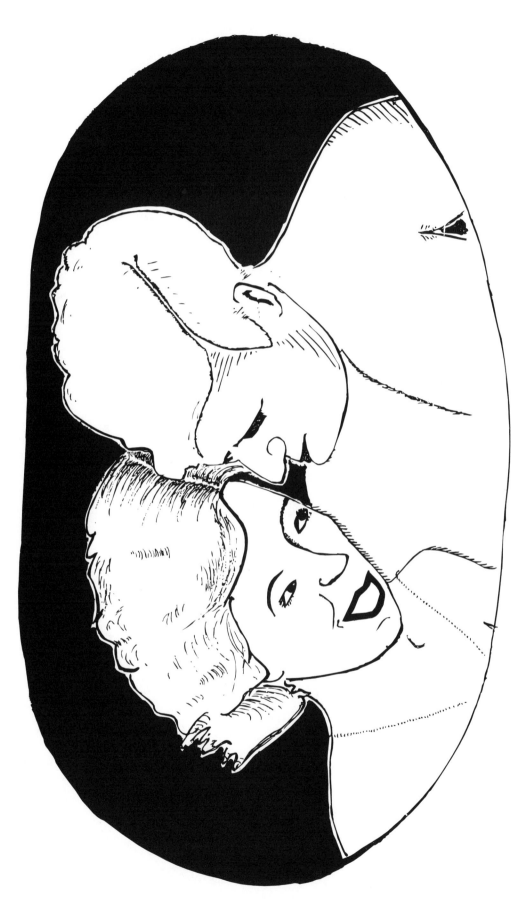

111

112

114

115

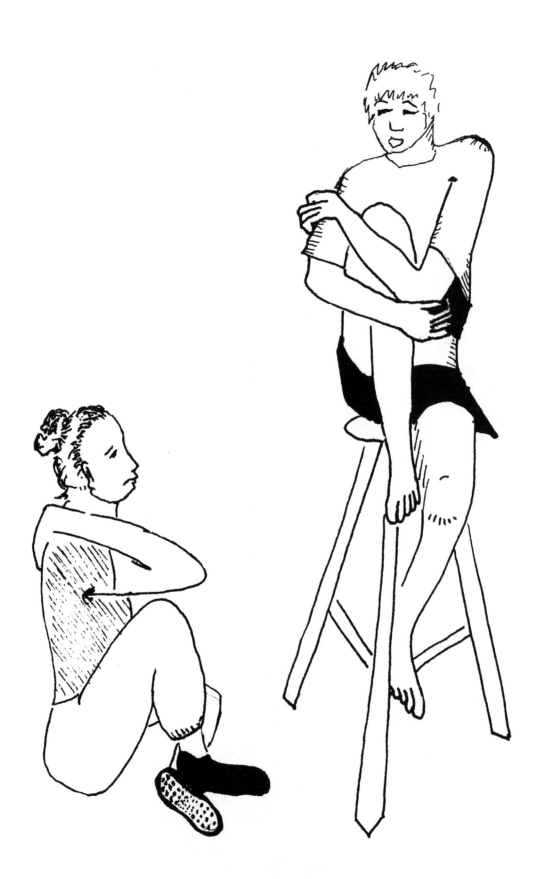

116

A HAPPY COUPLE

ADAPTATIONS FOR SESSION 10

For Nonreaders and Nonwriters

4. Occasionallly there is a child who can't think of any couple who seems happy. I tell that child to make up an imaginary couple.

    For all the children, I reread the list to help them think of ways to draw their pictures.

For Older Children

4. These children can label their pictures by writing who the people are and what they are doing.

For Classroom Groups

This activity does not need modification.

Review

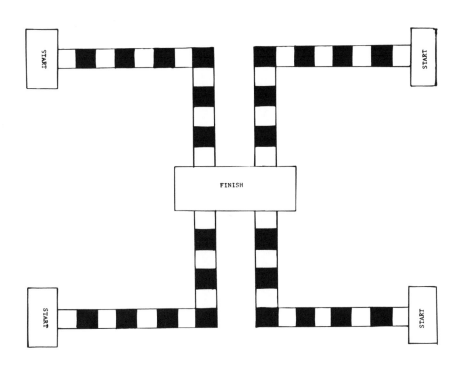

SESSION 11   LESSON PLAN

Aim: To review concepts, issues, and feelings about divorce.

Materials: Any game on the market about divorce

Or

The two sets of cards following this lesson with any suitable game board from a game you may already possess

Or

Create your own board to use with the cards following this lesson. Color the backs of one set of cards. Laminate all of them. Included is one possible board you can make. Alternate squares of two different colors to correspond with colors for each set of cards. Do something special when each player comes to the end, like everyone says something nice about the person who finishes. There is no winner. Each person gets a chance to finish.

Procedure: Play the game.

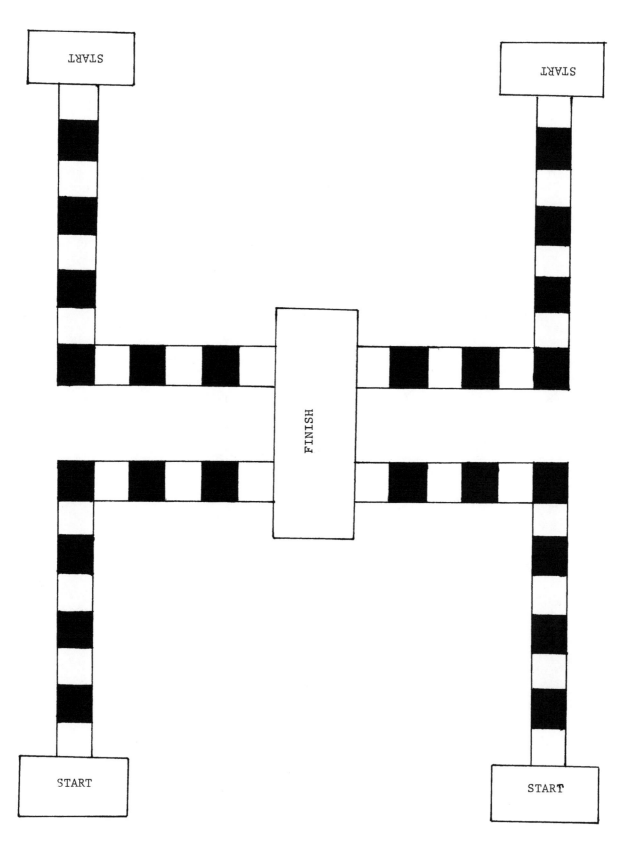

122

FIRST SET OF CARDS

A child hears his or her parents arguing. What are they arguing about?	What is one good thing about parents divorcing?
What is one good thing about parents remarrying?	What is one way a child's life can change when his or her parents separate?
What is one reason people choose to marry?	What is one reason people choose to divorce?
What is one way that you can tell that a couple has a happy marriage?	Tell one way your life has changed for the better since the divorce.

A boy was sitting at his desk, staring. What was he thinking about?	If someone who was invisible watched your family at home before the divorce, what would that person see?
Tell one way your life has changed for the worse since the divorce.	If someone who was invisible watched your family at home after the divorce, what would that person see?
When someone is grieving over his or her parents' divorce, how might he or she be feeling?	If someone who was invisible watched your family at home at the present time, what would that person see?
What is one way you have felt as a result of your parents' divorce, and when do you feel this way?	What is one good thing about your mom and dad not living together?

Say something good about your mother.	Say something good about your father.
Say something good about your family in the future.	Do you have a friend whose parents divorced? Who? How does that friend feel?
Who can you talk to about your parents' separation?	What is your biggest problem about the separation or divorce?
What is one thing you like to do with your dad?	What is one thing you like to do with your mom?

Say something the way your mother would say it.	Say something the way your father would say it.
What is one thing you wish for?	Tell something that happened to you recently that made you feel loved.
A fortune teller has just told you your fortune. What did he/she say?	Tell something that happened to you recently that made you feel unloved.
If you could change one thing in your life, what would it be?	A girl's mother has had to return to work after a separation, and can't spend as much time with her daughter as she once did. What could you say to her daughter to make her feel better?

©1996 by Sylvia Margolin

126

A boy's mother has started to go out on dates, and the boy is jealous. What could the mother say to him to make him feel better?	A boy who had always been well behaved in school starts acting up after his parents separate. He thinks this will make them feel guilty and therefore get back together. What advice would you give him?
A girl keeps asking her father when he and her mother are getting back together. What does the father answer?	A girl's mother's boyfriend tries to be nice to the girl when he comes to visit, but the girl ignores him. What advice would you give her?
A boy's dad has visitation rights, but hardly ever visits. What advice would you give the boy?	A girl is having trouble concentrating on her schoolwork. She keeps daydreaming about her parents getting back together. What advice would you give her?
A boy visits his father and keeps hearing him say the divorce was all his mother's fault. What could the boy say to his father?	A girl kept hearing her parents argue about how to raise her. She feels it's her fault when they finally separate. What advice could you give her?

SECOND SET OF CARDS

Jump up and down five times.	Make a funny face.
Hop on one foot across the room.	Shake hands with each person in the group.
Pat your head and rub your belly at the same time.	Close your eyes and spin around three times.
Walk around the room (or table) with this card on your head.	Skip in place while clapping your hands.

Make a scary sound.	Laugh.
Play patty-cake with the person on your left.	Walk across the room backward.
Close your eyes and touch the tip of your nose with a finger from each hand.	Wink five times with each eye.
Try to touch your nose with the tip of your tongue.	Snore.

Hold your nose and talk with a nasal voice.	Blink ten times.
What is your favorite color?	What is your favorite animal? Why?
What is your favorite season? Why?	What is your favorite TV show?
What is your favorite movie?	What is your favorite subject in school?

What is your least favorite subject in school?	What is your favorite thing to do?
What is your favorite song?	What is your favorite holiday? Why?
Who is your favorite movie star or singer?	What is your favorite toy or game?
What is your favorite dessert?	What is your favorite food?

If you could go anywhere in the world, where would you go? Why?	If you could spend a day with anyone, who would it be? Why?
What age would you want to be? Why?	If you were moving and could take only one possession with you, what would it be? Why?
Count backward from ten.	Say the letters of the alphabet as fast as you can.
Recite one nursery rhyme as fast as you can.	Count up to 100 by 10's.

©1996 by Sylvia Margolin

ADAPTATIONS FOR SESSION 11

For Nonreaders and Nonwriters

Read the cards aloud.

For Older Children

This activity does not need modification.

For Classroom Groups

If a student selects a card with a question that does not pertain to her or his situation (e.g., a student from an intact family chooses a card asking about one change that occurred in the family as a result of the divorce), have the child choose another card or rephrase the question so it fits the child's situation (e.g., tell about one big change that happened in his or her family.)

Termination: Achieving Closure

Aside from the usual tasks required of children in growing up, the children of divorce have additional tasks. Judith Wallerstein outlined six of these in a talk she gave in 1982 called, "Children of Divorce: The Psychological Tasks of the Child." Successful resolution of these tasks enables the children to achieve closure to the divorce experience.

Task 1: Acknowledging the Reality of the Marital Rupture

This task should be addressed at the time of the separation so that children have a clear and realistic understanding that their parents are separating and the reasons for it. Otherwise their fantasies run rampant and are often worse than the reality. It often takes up to a year for children to master this task and accept, not the permanence of the separation, but its reality.

Task 2: Disengaging from Parental Conflict and Distress and Resuming Customary Pursuits

This task too should begin to be addressed immediately after the parents have separated. Essentially, it enables the children to separate from parental conflict in both inner and outer ways. The image of the ruptured marriage may be foremost within the children's consciousness, draining them of the energy they had previously used to learn, to socialize, and to recreate. On an outer level, they may be so busy attempting to reunite their separated parents, trying to get as much attention as they once received, or comforting a grieving parent that they are too busy to study, to meet with friends, or to play ball. The task for them is to disengage from the parent conflict and to focus on their own lives. The successful resolution of this task enables the children to reestablish their earlier levels of learning and to engage once again in age-appropriate activities. It, like the first task, is usually mastered in the first year.

Task 3: Resolution of Loss

Wallerstein calls this the most difficult task because it requires overcoming profound losses such as parent, familiar routines, family traditions, and an intact family. Often the children feel that they are being rejected or that they are unlovable when a parent leaves, or that they are powerless beings, victims of unfortunate circumstances. Mastery of this task comes when children no longer feel victimized, but instead come to terms with the limitations and constraints of the single-parent or remarried family with whom they now live. This task takes longer to achieve than the first two. It is made easier when the noncustodial parent maintains regular visitation and a loving relationship. It is harder to master when children remain disappointed by an unreliable, disinterested, or absent parent.

Task 4: Resolving Anger and Self-Blame

Because people, rather than nature, are responsible for divorce, children who are angry tend to blame one or the other parent or themselves for causing it. They may target their anger at the parent who requested the divorce, or they may blame both parents for caring only about themselves and for not considering the needs and wishes of the children. This anger, especially in older children, keeps them at a distance from their parent(s), and may become acting-out behavior in school and in the community. Children may also blame themselves for causing many of the arguments in the family. Later on, after the separation, they may be plagued with guilt regarding wishes they once had for their battling parents to divorce. Or they may blame themselves for failing to restore the marriage. The anger diminishes as the children gain a more expansive and realistic sense of each of their parents and the reasons for the divorce. This may lead to their being able to forgive the person with whom they were angry and reconcile the relationship.

Task 5: Accepting the Permanence of the Divorce

It is more difficult for children of divorce to achieve this task than for bereaved children. The latter know that death is permanent, but children of divorce see their parents and can easily imagine them living together again. The reality of the permanence seeps in very gradually over years, but is made more difficult when one parent continues to hope for reunion.

Task 6: Achieving Realistic Hope Regarding Relationships

The successful resolution of the five preceding tasks makes it more probable that this last task will be achieved as well. Many young people from divorced families are frightened that they may repeat the marital failure they experienced in their own lives. They must take the risk in the hope that they can sustain a loving union while at the same time fearing they may fail.

The adjustment the family makes to the divorce greatly influences how successful children will be in mastering these six tasks. If the parents have resolved their conflicts following the divorce, if both parents continue to maintain loving relationships with their children, and if the quality of life is positive, then mastery is likely. On the other hand, if the family remains in conflict, in litigation, in a state of disequilibrium, children are greatly hindered in their attempts to reach closure.

SESSION 12 LESSON PLAN

Aim: 1. To compare ideas and feelings with those from the first group session.

2. To terminate with positive feelings.

Materials: 1. "Ideas About Divorce: Post-Test" worksheet

2. All the completed worksheets from previous sessions

3. "Certificate of Achievement" worksheet

4. Pencils

5. Large sheet of construction paper

6. Crayons or markers or colored pencils

Procedure: 1. Say, "This is our last session. Let's see if your ideas and feelings have changed since the time we started the group." Distribute "Ideas About Divorce" worksheet. Leader will read aloud, and group members will complete the post-test.

2. Distribute the original pretest version of this worksheet for members to compare. Say, "Look at those items that show a big change from the first time you filled this out." Those who wish may share some of these.

3. Distribute one large sheet of construction paper to each group member to be used as a cover for a book of all the papers they've completed during the course of the group. Have the children fold it in half. On the front, they can name their book (Example: My Family's Divorce, Feelings About Divorce, Children of Divorce, etc.) and write their names as authors. Then, they can draw a picture on the cover.

4. Distribute "Certificate of Achievement" worksheets that have been filled out for each child. While the children are working on the covers, leader can go around and staple in all the completed worksheets including the "Certificate of Achievement." The books are now ready for the children to take home and show to parents.

Closing: See #10 from the list. Pass around a handshake, a linked elbow, a silly face, a food treat that is placed directly into a neighbor's mouth, and a hug.

Name _____ Date _____

IDEAS ABOUT DIVORCE
(Post-test)

Directions: Check to show how you feel at this time.

	NEVER	SOMETIMES	USUALLY	ALWAYS
1. Divorce is a very bad experience.				
2. When people marry, they should stay married.				
3. Divorce is better than having parents argue all the time.				
4. Life stays pretty much the same for kids after the divorce as it was before the divorce.				
5. When parents get divorced, it can be the children's fault.				
6. I like visiting the parent I don't live with.				
7. I can talk about the divorce with my parents, relatives, or friends and they will listen and understand me.				
8. Parents should get married again after a divorce.				
9. Stepparents are usually mean to the children.				
10. I feel sad and angry about the divorce.				

CERTIFICATE OF ACHIEVEMENT

AWARDED TO

_____

FOR COMPLETING A TWELVE-WEEK GROUP FOR CHILDREN OF DIVORCE

DATE _____ FACILITATOR _____

ADAPTATIONS FOR SESSION 12

For Nonreaders and Nonwriters

2. Leader will focus on one child at a time and select one or two items that have changed the most and comment on these.

3. Write the possible names for the books on a sheet of construction paper or on a blackboard so the children can copy one.

For Older Children

This activity does not need modification.

For Classroom Groups

1 and 2. Omit.

3. Possible names for books may be "About Families," "My Family," "A Book About the _____ (name) Family."

Case Studies

Two brothers, Timothy in fifth grade and Jason in fourth, live with their natural father, his girlfriend, and two younger sisters. The boys' natural parents were separated about a year and a half before the group started. According to father, he was in the navy and when he returned, mother was dating someone else. Mother left the house, and father quit the navy to take care of the children. He got a new job out of state and the family moved. The children have not seen their mother since the move. There are some letters and phone calls, but not on a consistent basis. The father's phone number was unlisted, and he would not give it to the childrens' mother until she started making child support payments.

During the course of the group, I spoke with dad a number of times about the children's need for contact with mother. Because he was reasonable and open to doing what was best for the children, despite his fury with his ex-wife, he began divorce proceedings and worked out an agreement to get child support in exchange for regular phone and in-person visits. By the time the group ended, the parents had divorced, father had remarried, and the children were very much looking forward to spending two weeks with their mother in the summertime.

Jason, the younger brother, is a good student, has some friends, and, according to dad and teacher, seems well adjusted. Timothy often fails subjects on his report card because he does not turn in completed work, and he is rejected by peers for "being gross," performing behaviors like picking his nose and putting staples in his mouth.

In the first session, Timothy spoke about the initial separation of his parents: "Our real mother didn't live with us when Dad came back from overseas. One night she suddenly came and said she was leaving. I didn't know what she meant." Jason spoke a lot. This is part of the story he told: "One day I was sitting on the couch and Mom called. My sister said I'll be surprised. I took the phone, said hello, and yelled 'Yippee!' . . . ." The central issue for both of these boys appears to be the loss and separation from mother.

Ideas About Divorce Pretest

Both Timothy and Jason did not respond to item 6 about visiting the noncustodial parent. The rest of their responses are identical except for the last two. Jason is more realistic in thinking his parents will not reunite and more in touch with his grieving feelings.

IDEAS ABOUT DIVORCE

Pretest by Timothy

Directions: Check to show how you feel at this time.

	NEVER	SOMETIMES	USUALLY	ALWAYS
1. Divorce is a very bad experience.		X		
2. When people marry, they should stay married.				X
3. Divorce is better than having parents argue all the time.			X	
4. Life stays pretty much the same for kids after the divorce as it was before the divorce.		X		
5. When parents get divorced, it can be the children's fault.	X			
6. I like visiting the parent I don't live with.				
7. I can talk about the divorce with my parents, relatives, or friends and they will listen and understand me.			X	
8. Parents should get married again after a divorce, to someone new.		X		
9. I think my parents will get back together again.		X		
10. I feel sad and angry about the divorce.		X		

IDEAS ABOUT DIVORCE

Pretest by Jason

Directions: Check to show how you feel at this time.

	NEVER	SOMETIMES	USUALLY	ALWAYS
1. Divorce is a very bad experience.		X		
2. When people marry, they should stay married.				X
3. Divorce is better than having parents argue all the time.			X	
4. Life stays pretty much the same for kids after the divorce as it was before the divorce.		X		
5. When parents get divorced, it can be the children's fault.	X			
6. I like visiting the parent I don't live with.				
7. I can talk about the divorce with my parents, relatives, or friends and they will listen and understand me.			X	
8. Parents should get married again after a divorce, to someone new.		X		
9. I think my parents will get back together again.	X			
10. I feel sad and angry about the divorce.				X

Family Album

A Happy Time with My Family. Timothy drew a picture of when he was born. The picture is very "me" centered. It is a time before his brother and the other siblings are born, and where he gets all the attention.

Jason's response is more typical. He drew a picture of mom, dad, the children and the grandparents all going to Busch Gardens together. There appears to be a wider support group in his world view.

An Unhappy Time with My Family. Timothy 's picture shows the family indoors. They were about to go on a picnic, but it rained heavily. His house seems heavy, the people in it are inaccessible.

In Jason's picture, he is crying because mother just left the family. In fact, mother is not presented in the drawing at all. Jason shows himself as being in touch with his feelings.

Why I Think My Parents Got Married. Both drew pictures of the time their parents met. Both said they married because they loved each other.

Why I Think My Parents Got Divorced. Timothy drew a picture of father out at sea. He said about his drawing that dad had most of the money. The kids had to stop taking karate lessons because mom didn't have enough money to pay for them. In actuality, most of dad's check was sent home to support the family. The boys were told that they could take only the few free trial lessons. With dad's help, this misinformation was clarified. Once again, Timothy shows himself as being heavily defended against seeing the truth and experiencing his feelings.

Jason is able to see things clearly and honestly. His picture shows the slamming door after a loud argument between Mom and Dad. Dad is saying, "If you're cheating on me, leave." Both say, "Fine." Once again, there is no mother in the picture.

How I Want the Future to Be in My Family. Both boys want their natural parents to become reunited. Timothy drew them remarrying. Jason drew them apologizing to each other.

Notice, however, that the father in Timothy's picture is full-bodied and has a neck and feet. The mother is just a stick figure without hair, a mouth, hands, or feet. She is barely there!

Jason again leaves mother out of the picture entirely! She is represented by a sun.

FAMILY ALBUM
by Timothy

A Happy Time with My Family

An Unhappy Time with My Family

Why I Think My Parents Got
Married

Why I Think My Parents Got
Separated/Divorced

What I Want the Future to Be
in My Family

FAMILY ALBUM
by Jason

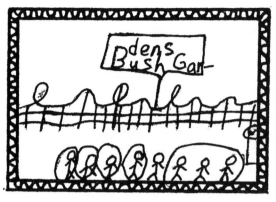

A Happy Time with My Family

An Unhappy Time with My Family

Why I Think My Parents Got
Married

Why I Think My Parents Got
Separated/Divorced

How I Want the Future to Be
in My Family

Changes

The issues with which the boys are dealing, aside from missing their mother, are very different. Timothy is aware that his grades are poor and that he has trouble getting along with peers. He probably meant to put a circle, not a heart, around the picture with the caption, "Having more arguments or fights with friends or classmates." Again, he shows himself without a strong support system, feeling the loss, not of mother this time, but of friends.

Jason is more in touch with the numerous changes that occurred following the parental breakup. For him, "Being alone or with a baby-sitter more because parent has to work" is a realistic issue, as dad works till 7:00 P.M. But he is looking forward to dad's remarrying and creating a stable home life. He is more optimistic and shows his need for family support.

CHANGES
by Timothy

152

CHANGES
by Jason (Page 1)

153

CHANGES
by Jason (Page 2)

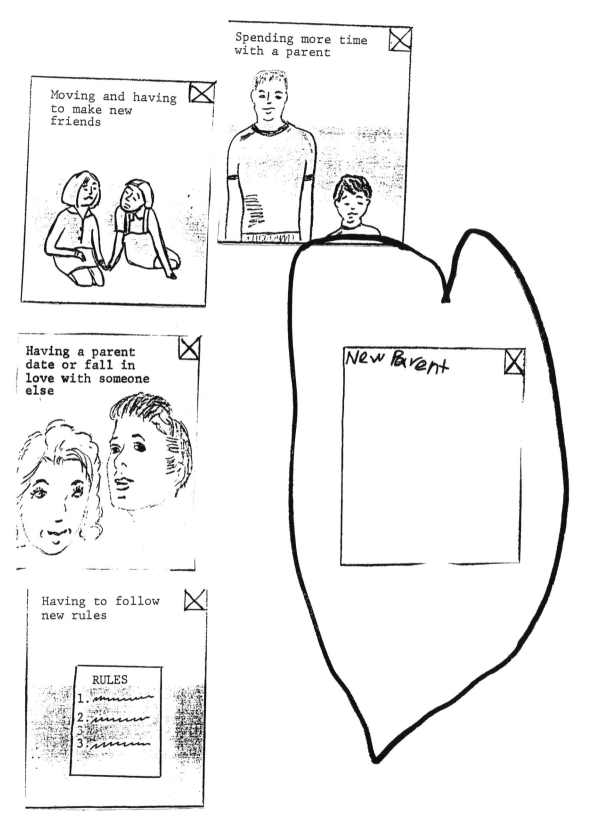

Spending more time with a parent

Moving and having to make new friends

Having a parent date or fall in love with someone else

Having to follow new rules

RULES
1.
2.
3.
3.

New Parent

154

People Who Live in My House

In these pictures, the two brothers show how competitive they are and how they take their anger out on each other. In Timothy's picture, Jason is the shortest, even smaller than the two younger sisters. In Jason's picture, Timothy is the only family member without a super-cape, a super-badge, and muscles. In addition, he is standing next to Timothy with more muscles than anyone, saying, "I'll stomp you!"[*]

Timothy's pictures convey a strong desire to live with mother. He alone has wings that enable him to take off like a rocket (note fire on the bottom of each one). He would leave this house of faceless, unsupportive people. On the worksheet "Family Members Who Don't Live with Me," he shows a marked division of space. Mother is walking up steps away from her boyfriend. There are also numerous items on the roof, and, according to most books on art therapy, this conveys a very active fantasy life. Two of the items are chimneys; one is an antenna, and one looks like an alien, perhaps Timothy himself, wanting to be present! It is interesting to note that though mother and her boyfriend have faces, unlike the family members with whom Timothy lives, they have spindly stick-figure bodies. There doesn't seem to be much support in this house either.

Jason, for the first and only time in all his drawings uses stick figures to draw mother and her boyfriend on the worksheet, "Family Members Who Don't Live with Me." In addition, mom doesn't even have a nose or mouth as the boyfriend does. She's barely there at all!

[*]Throughout the Case Studies, labels were added by the author to the children's art for one of two reasons: Children omitted labels in their pictures, or names were replaced by labels indicating the relationships of the person to the child.

PEOPLE WHO LIVE IN MY HOUSE
by Timothy

FAMILY MEMBERS WHO DON'T LIVE WITH ME
by Timothy

PEOPLE WHO LIVE IN MY HOUSE
by Jason

FAMILY MEMBERS WHO DON'T LIVE WITH ME
by Jason

159

The Grieving Process

Jason describes himself as having just about equal amounts of all the feelings, except guilt.

Timothy used to have all these feelings, including guilt, but, he is saying he no longer does. Now, he primarily feels sad and angry since the breakup of his parents' marriage, but there are growing amounts of hope and acceptance. This picture shows a significant change for the better in Timothy. He is more in touch with the real feelings that are there.

A Happy Marriage

The two brothers both chose to draw pictures of dad and his girlfriend, who were married shortly after this session. Timothy drew them going on a bike ride together. He continues to show improvement. In his picture, he draws a foreground, and the two adults are firmly planted on it. The picture shows that he is feeling more grounded and solid. Notice, however, that the tandem bicycle is powered by rocket fuel. Does he want them to take off?

Jason chose to draw his father and girlfriend sailing on a boat. The adults are not grounded here. At opposite sides of the boat, with their arms outstretched, it looks as if they are flailing and calling for help.

THE GRIEVING PROCESS
by Timothy

THE GRIEVING PROCESS
by Jason

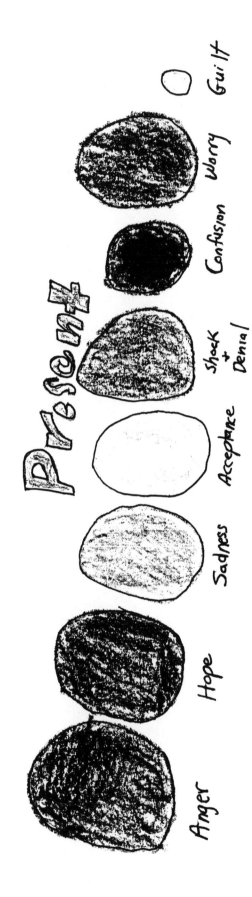

Anger • Hope • Sadness • Acceptance • Shock + Denial • Confusion • Worry • Guilt

Present

162

A HAPPY MARRIAGE
by Timothy

163

A HAPPY MARRIAGE
by Jason

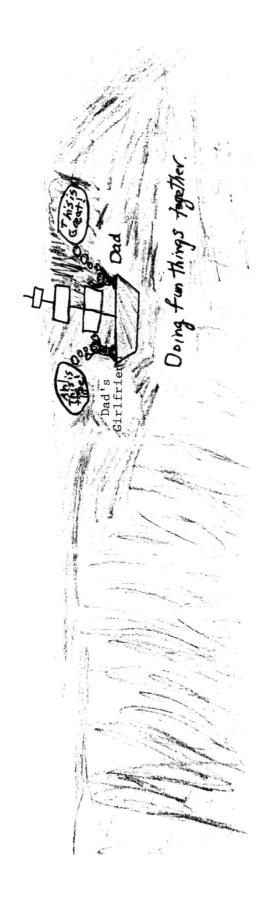

164

Ideas About Divorce Post-test

One major change for both boys is that they now have responded to item 6. Even though they still have not visited with mom, they both are looking forward to it.

Also, both responded quite differently from the pretest to item 1. Whereas before, they checked that divorce is *sometimes* a very bad experience, at the conclusion of the group, they both were more fully aware of how difficult the marital break up has been for them. They both responded by checking that divorce is *always* a very bad experience.

Timothy appears to have become more defended once again. He indicates that he *rarely* has strong feelings about the divorce. But he is more realistic in checking that his parents will *never* get back together.

IDEAS ABOUT DIVORCE
Post-test by Timothy

Directions: Check to show how you feel at this time.

	NEVER	SOMETIMES	USUALLY	ALWAYS
1. Divorce is a very bad experience.				X
2. When people marry, they should stay married.				X
3. Divorce is better than having parents argue all the time.		X		
4. Life stays pretty much the same for kids after the divorce as it was before the divorce.		X		
5. When parents get divorced, it can be the children's fault.	X			
6. I like visiting the parent I don't live with.				X
7. I can talk about the divorce with my parents, relatives, or friends and they will listen and understand me.				X
8. Parents should get married again after a divorce, to someone new.		X		
9. I think my parents will get back together again.	X			
10. I feel sad and angry about the divorce.	*rarely*			

©1996 by Sylvia Margolin

166

IDEAS ABOUT DIVORCE
Post-test by Jason

Directions: Check to show how you feel at this time.

	NEVER	SOMETIMES	USUALLY	ALWAYS
1. Divorce is a very bad experience.				X
2. When people marry, they should stay married.			X	
3. Divorce is better than having parents argue all the time.				X
4. Life stays pretty much the same for kids after the divorce as it was before the divorce.	X			
5. When parents get divorced, it can be the children's fault.	X			
6. I like visiting the parent I don't live with.				X
7. I can talk about the divorce with my parents, relatives, or friends and they will listen and understand me.				X
8. Parents should get married again after a divorce, to someone new.		X		
9. I think my parents will get back together again.	X			
10. I feel sad and angry about the divorce.				X

CASE STUDY OF TWO SISTERS

Mindy and Alissa are two sisters who live with their father, his girlfriend, an older sister in fifth grade, and a younger brother who does not yet attend school. A half brother with a different father is now living with mother. Mindy is in fourth grade and Alissa is in first.

Their parents were separated about three years before the group started. Their older sister had been in a group previously, and mother requested that these two children be included at this time. Mother was in the process of moving to her own apartment, starting divorce proceedings, and filing for custody. She said Mindy, the fourth grader, was adjusting well, but the younger Alissa was very sad and having a hard time concentrating on her schoolwork.

According to mother, she and her husband were arguing and not getting along for quite a while before mother left the house. She continued to see the children fairly regularly, but often they had to take turns because there were so many of them. She moved into her own apartment shortly after the group started. After a few initial joyous visits, the children have rarely seen their mom because she lost her job and has had money and car problems so she could not pick them up.

Father and his girlfriend of about a year have had problems getting along and the latter is planning to move out when she can afford to set up her own apartment.

In the first session, when asked, in an open-ended way, to tell the group something about the family situation, Mindy, the older girl, told this story: "I live with my dad and my two sisters and one brother. My mom moved out because they kept on fighting. Later on my mom took Allen [older brother] to my grandmother's house. I would like my mom to move back in and for them to stop fighting." This theme of reunification crops up for Mindy throughout the sessions. Part of this fantasy derives from her dissatisfaction with dad's girlfriend. During the check-ins, Mindy spoke about feeling good that the girlfriend was moving out because she is mean, not to her, but to the other three children in the house. She chose to role play two scenes for the activity on anger in session 5: dad and mom fighting, and dad's girlfriend threatening to put a lock on the phone so the children couldn't call mom so often. The incident Mindy selected that she remembered most from the filmstrip we watched in session 6 was the girl in the story talking to the father about feeling angry at the father's new girlfriend for being bossy.

When asked, in the first session, to tell something about the family, Alissa, the first grader, told this story: "I don't live with my mom. Dad and Mom kept on fighting. We went downstairs by my uncle where it wasn't noisy. One day cops came. There was too much fighting. And then Mom moved to Grandma's house. She comes back and picks us up every weekend."

For Alissa, there are two central themes. One is for dad to marry so she can have a mother. Her first choice would be for him to remarry mom, but it would be better to have dad's girlfriend for a mom than none at all. During some check-ins she spoke about her mother in glowing terms after she returned from a visit to mom's new apartment. During the last few sessions, she talked about feeling very sad because she hadn't seen her mom in weeks. For check-ins at other times she spoke about dad's girlfriend, usually with ambivalence: Dad's girlfriend was mean, but she gave her dessert; she was getting to sleep on time now, but sometimes dad's girlfriend was cooking too late. The scene Alissa remembered most from the filmstrip was the father in the story saying that he and his girlfriend were getting married.

The other theme that concerns Alissa is the frequency and intensity of conflict in her family throughout her life. She made indirect reference to the violence she witnessed between her natural father and mother in the very first session. Secondary are the battles between the children, or between parent and child. In session 5 on anger, Alissa chose to role play a scene where mom was screaming at the kids because they didn't clean their room and because they were fighting with each other. Her most unhappy memory, as recorded in session 2, was dad sending her to her room because her bed was messed up.

Ideas About Divorce Pretest

Alissa again shows concern about the arguing of her parents. Even though she indicates in item 2 that people should always stay married, in 3 she says that divorce is better than arguing. Both girls have strong reunification fantasies three years after their parents have separated. Both indicated that they always think their parents will get back together again.

Family Album

A Happy Time with My Family. Mindy drew a picture of her dad getting off an airplane, coming home from the navy. Mom was there to greet him and bring him back home. Most children, like Mindy, draw pictures of a happy time when their parents were together.

Alissa drew her older brother and herself jumping on the bed and said she likes to play fight with him. He had recently moved out to live with mother, so Alissa was experiencing another loss.

An Unhappy Time with My Family. Mindy drew her mom leaving in her station wagon. Again, most children draw a picture of the initial breakup.

Alissa drew dad sending her to her room. She said it was because her brother messed it up and she had to clean it. The jumping-on-bed incident probably just happened, so it was fresh in her mind, yet it shows how disturbing any form of conflict is for her.

Why I Think My Parents Got Married. Both girls drew pictures illustrating that their parents loved each other. The child in their pictures is Allen, the oldest boy, who was around at the time.

Why I Think My Parents Got Separated/Divorced. Mindy drew her parents arguing a lot. Note how much larger mom is than dad, and the word "yell" in her balloon is distinct while dad's word is blurred.

Alissa said about her picture, "Mom always called a girl, I mean a man she liked. Also they got into a lot of fights." Her picture shows mom leaving in the car. Note how mom has no arms in this frame, and how both parents had no arms in the preceding frame.

How I Want the Future to Be in My Family. Mindy drew a picture of dad running out of the house to see mom.

Alissa said she wants mom to live with dad and sleep in his green bed with him. Both girls seem to have very vivid fantasies about their parents reuniting.

IDEAS ABOUT DIVORCE
Pretest by Mindy

Directions: Check to show how you feel at this time.

	NEVER	SOMETIMES	USUALLY	ALWAYS
1. Divorce is a very bad experience.		X		
2. When people marry, they should stay married.			X	
3. Divorce is better than having parents argue all the time.	X			
4. Life stays pretty much the same for kids after the divorce as it was before the divorce.		X		
5. When parents get divorced, it can be the children's fault.	X			
6. I like visiting the parent I don't live with.				X
7. I can talk about the divorce with my parents, relatives, or friends and they will listen and understand me.		X		
8. Parents should get married again after a divorce, to someone new.		X		
9. I think my parents will get back together again.				X
10. I feel sad and angry about the divorce.		X		

IDEAS ABOUT DIVORCE

Pretest by Alissa

Directions: Check to show how you feel at this time.

	NEVER	SOMETIMES	USUALLY	ALWAYS
1. Divorce is a very bad experience.		X		
2. When people marry, they should stay married.				X
3. Divorce is better than having parents argue all the time.				X
4. Life stays pretty much the same for kids after the divorce as it was before the divorce.		X		
5. When parents get divorced, it can be the children's fault.	X			
6. I like visiting the parent I don't live with.				X
7. I can talk about the divorce with my parents, relatives, or friends and they will listen and understand me.	X			
8. Parents should get married again after a divorce, to someone new.				X
9. I think my parents will get back together again.				X
10. I feel sad and angry about the divorce.				X

FAMILY ALBUM
by Mindy

A Happy Time with My Family

An Unhappy Time with My Family

Why I Think My Parents Got
Married

Why I Think My Parents Got
Separated/Divorced

How I Want the Future to Be
in My Family

173

FAMILY ALBUM
by Alissa

A Happy Time with My Family

An Unhappy Time with My Family

Why I Think My Parents Got
Married

Why I Think My Parents Got
Separated/Divorced

How I Want the Future to Be
in My Family

Changes

Both sisters' responses to the exercise on "Changes" were remarkably similar. They each chose eight frames to include, and seven out of the eight are the same for each of them. In addition, they both circled, "Having to follow new rules" as the one change that has made their lives better since the separation.

Since the first group session, both girls have conveyed that their major desire is for their parents to get back together again. Therefore, when asked to circle the one change that has upset them the most as a result of their parents' separation, they both circled, "Having a parent date or fall in love with someone else." Since both parents are seeing other people, the girls see this as a major obstacle to reunification.

Because she is strongly grieving the loss of her mother, Alissa added, "Spending less time with one or both parents." Both girls show, in these activities, that they are in touch with reality and with their feelings.

CHANGES
by Mindy

Not having as much arguing and fighting in the house

Having a parent date or fall in love with someone else

Having to live in two different places

Having to follow new rules

Being alone or with a babysitter more because parent needs to work

Eating either too much or too little

Having more responsibilities

Spending less time with one or both parents

176

CHANGES
by Alissa

Spending less time with one or both parents

Having more responsibilities

Having to live in two different places

Not having as much arguing and fighting in the house

Being alone or with a babysitter more because parent needs to work

Having more, arguments or fights with brothers and sisters

Having a parent date or fall in love with someone else

Having to follow new rules

RULES
1. ⌇⌇⌇⌇
2. ⌇⌇⌇⌇
3. ⌇⌇⌇⌇

People Who Live in My House

Both girls responded to this activity by appropriately including all family members in one of the two houses. There are a few interesting details to note.

Mindy placed all the siblings except herself to the left of father and his girlfriend. In Alissa's drawing, Mindy is alone at the top of the house with father. Mindy is a good girl who does well in school, is quiet, does not get into arguments with adults or children in the family.

In Alissa's drawing, the little brother is standing on the bureau! The older sister, who does much of the child care, is standing next to him. Alissa has separated dad from his girlfriend and placed herself next to the girlfriend. She sorely misses having a mother. She drew herself somewhat out of the boundary line of the house, but in the worksheet "Family Members Who Don't Live with Me," she drew about a third of mother's form outside the house boundary! Mother belongs with her. There should not be house boundaries to separate them. Also, notice all the lights and even the sun shining within mother's house.

PEOPLE WHO LIVE IN MY HOUSE
by Mindy

Cat

Younger Sister Alissa · Older Sister · Younger Brother · Father · Father's Girlfriend · Mindy

FAMILY MEMBERS WHO DON'T LIVE WITH ME
by Mindy

Mother

Older Brother

Cat

PEOPLE WHO LIVE IN MY HOUSE
by Alissa

Older
Sister
Mindy

Father

Father's
Girlfriend

Alissa

Oldest
Sister

Younger
Brother

FAMILY MEMBERS WHO DON'T LIVE WITH ME
by Alissa

Cat

Older
Brother

Mother

182

The Grieving Process

Both girls describe themselves in this activity as having very strong feelings of grief. Sadness, three years after their parents separated, is still the strongest emotion for each of them. Alissa also included a large red circle of anger, almost as large as the blue circle of sadness. Mindy, however, along with her grieving feelings, included a large yellow triangle symbolizing acceptance, the first time she has indicated this feeling.

Worry is another strong emotion they both feel. There is still so much that is unresolved in their family situation. The parents still have not gotten a divorce. They are renewing their battles more intensely than ever in their fight to get custody of the children. Mother just ended a relationship with one man and started one with another. She is out of work and hasn't the money to pick the children up for a visit. Father is about to end a relationship he's had for about a year. The family is still so unstable, and the girls are worried about their own welfare as well as their parents' lives.

THE GRIEVING PROCESS
by Mindy

THE GRIEVING PROCESS
by Alissa (Page 1)

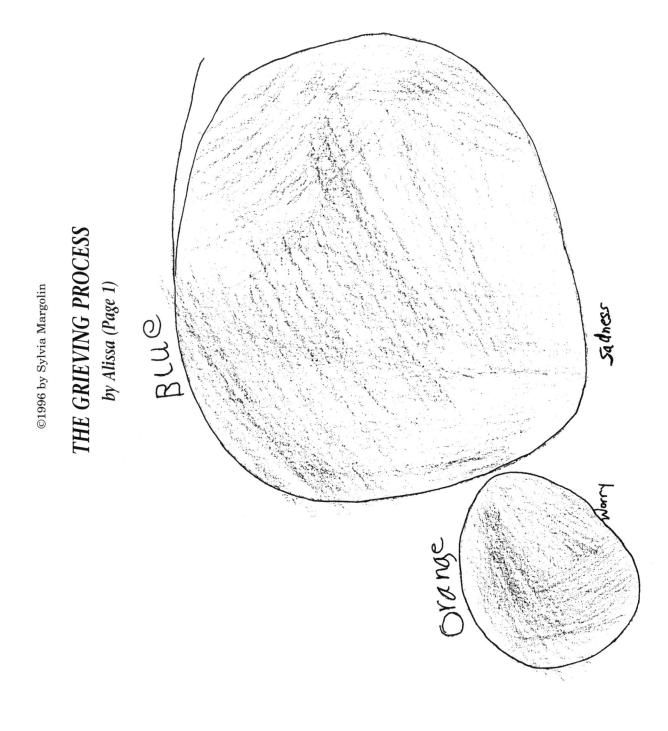

Blue

Sadness

Orange

Worry

185

THE GRIEVING PROCESS
by Alissa (Page 2)

Anger

©1996 by Sylvia Margolin

A Happy Marriage

Alissa was absent on the day we did this activity. Mindy chose to draw a picture of her neighbors and their daughter celebrating the daughter's birthday together. She said this couple never fights, seems happy, and goes to places together like the community pool and the pizza restaurant.

Mindy's wish for a close family comes through very strongly in this picture. The parents are celebrating an event for their one daughter. They are all snuggled closely together on the couch, even though there is plenty of sitting space in the room.

A HAPPY MARRIAGE
by Mindy

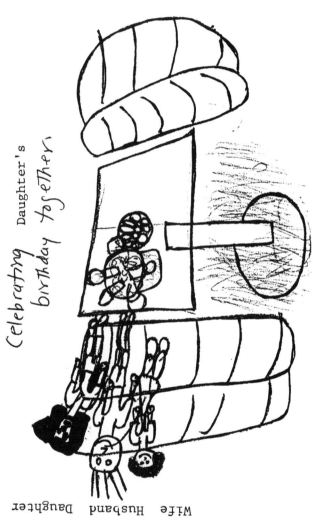

Celebrating Daughter's birthday together

Wife Husband Daughter

188

Ideas About Divorce Post-test

The responses of both sisters remained almost the same on this post-test as they were on the pretest except for two major areas.

Item 7 changed radically, perhaps because of being in the group. Both checked that they now can always talk about the separation to people and be understood. In the pretest, Alissa said she could *never* talk about the family situation, and Mindy said she *sometimes* could.

Even more significant, in response to item 9, both girls checked that now they *never* think their parents will get back together. On the pretest, both wrote that they *always* think their parents will reunite. Sometime during the course of the group, they both began to accept the reality of the parental separation.

IDEAS ABOUT DIVORCE
Post-test by Mindy

Directions: Check to show how you feel at this time.

	NEVER	SOMETIMES	USUALLY	ALWAYS
1. Divorce is a very bad experience.		X		
2. When people marry, they should stay married.			X	
3. Divorce is better than having parents argue all the time.				X
4. Life stays pretty much the same for kids after the divorce as it was before the divorce.		X		
5. When parents get divorced, it can be the children's fault.	X			
6. I like visiting the parent I don't live with.				X
7. I can talk about the divorce with my parents, relatives, or friends and they will listen and understand me.				X
8. Parents should get married again after a divorce, to someone new.			X	
9. I think my parents will get back together again.	X			
10. I feel sad and angry about the divorce.		X		

IDEAS ABOUT DIVORCE
Post-test by Alissa

Directions: Check to show how you feel at this time.

	NEVER	SOMETIMES	USUALLY	ALWAYS
1. Divorce is a very bad experience.		X		
2. When people marry, they should stay married.		X		
3. Divorce is better than having parents argue all the time.	X			
4. Life stays pretty much the same for kids after the divorce as it was before the divorce.		X		
5. When parents get divorced, it can be the children's fault.	X			
6. I like visiting the parent I don't live with.				X
7. I can talk about the divorce with my parents, relatives, or friends and they will listen and understand me.				X
8. Parents should get married again after a divorce, to someone new.		X		
9. I think my parents will get back together again.	X			
10. I feel sad and angry about the divorce.				X

191

CASE STUDY OF A SECOND-GRADE GIRL

Lisa is a second grader who lives with her natural father, older brother, and younger sister. Also sharing the house are an aunt, uncle, cousin, and cousin's girlfriend. Lisa's parents were divorced four years before the group started. Her teacher made the referral because Lisa talked often about missing her mother, and, in the teacher's words, "wouldn't eat lunch today and cried during recess."

According to both the aunt and the father, mother was and is an alcoholic who, while still living with Lisa's father, began seeing other men. Lisa sees mom every couple of weeks for the weekend, but it is not consistent. When she returns from a visit, she often has temper tantrums.

In the first session, when asked to tell something about her family, Lisa said, "I want my mom to move back in. I miss her a lot." During the course of the group at check-in time, she almost always talked about anticipating a visit or an actual visit with mom.

Ideas About Divorce Pretest

Lisa is still very much mourning the loss of her mother. She checked that she *usually* feels sad and angry about the divorce. In addition, probably because the divorce occurred when she was about four, there are still remnants of guilt as indicated in item 5.

IDEAS ABOUT DIVORCE
Pretest by Lisa

Directions: Check to show how you feel at this time.

	NEVER	SOMETIMES	USUALLY	ALWAYS
1. Divorce is a very bad experience.			X	
2. When people marry, they should stay married.		X		
3. Divorce is better than having parents argue all the time.		X		
4. Life stays pretty much the same for kids after the divorce as it was before the divorce.			X	
5. When parents get divorced, it can be the children's fault.		X		
6. I like visiting the parent I don't live with.				X
7. I can talk about the divorce with my parents, relatives, or friends and they will listen and understand me.				X
8. Parents should get married again after a divorce, to someone new.		X		
9. I think my parents will get back together again.	X			
10. I feel sad and angry about the divorce.			X	

Family Album

A Happy Time with My Family. Lisa drew herself opening a present on her birthday.

An Unhappy Time with My Family. Lisa drew her mom moving out. Notice, however, that both parents are smiling during this intensely emotional occasion.

Why I Think My Parents Got Married. Lisa drew her parents in love with each other. Notice, however, that dad is frowning—anticipating, perhaps, how the marriage will end.

Why I Think My Parents Got Separated/Divorced. Lisa drew mom at a party where she stayed too late. "She didn't come home till 12:30." Notice how both mom and the balloons are flying. At this point in the group, we began to talk about mom's alcohol problem. Would parents really get divorced if one of them came home a little late one time? Did mom go to parties and bars often? Lisa said yes. Did she sometimes stay out all night long? Lisa said yes. Did she sometimes come home drunk? Lisa said yes.

How I Want the Future to Be in My Family. Lisa drew a picture of the entire family together again. She said, "I want them to get back together but know they won't." Once again, there is an unhappy mouth on mom when one would expect it to be happy. This probably reflects the fact that Lisa knows the reunification won't happen.

Changes

Lisa selected eleven changes that occurred in her life since the divorce. She does appreciate that there is not as much arguing in the house. The change that upset her the most was moving and having to change schools. Change and loss of friends probably touches off the feelings of loss for mother.

People Who Live in My House

Notice how united Lisa drew her family, but how scattered are the people in her extended family. She would like nothing better than for them to leave and for mom to move back. Her picture of mom on the page "Family Members Who Don't Live with Me," is without feet, floating, without the foreground she drew on the first picture.

FAMILY ALBUM
by Lisa

A Happy Time with My Family

An Unhappy Time with My Family

Why I Think My Parents Got
Married

Why I Think My Parents Got
Separated/Divorced

How I Want the Future to Be
in My Family

CHANGES
by Lisa (Page 1)

196

CHANGES
by Lisa (Page 2)

Spending less time with one or both parents

Having a parent date or fall in love with someone else

Spending more time with a parent

Not having as much arguing and fighting in the house

Moving and having to change schools

Having less money

PEOPLE WHO LIVE IN MY HOUSE
by Lisa

cats

Cousin's
Girlfriend

Brother   Lisa   Dad   Sister   Cousin   Uncle Aunt

198

FAMILY MEMBERS WHO DON'T LIVE WITH ME
by Lisa

A Happy Marriage

Lisa was absent for the session on the grieving process. She drew a picture of another aunt and uncle whom she sees as having a happy marriage, not the aunt and uncle with whom she lives. They are celebrating a birthday together.

Ideas About Divorce Post-test

The biggest shift from the pretest is in item 3. On the pretest, Lisa checked that it is *sometimes* better to get divorced when parents argue all the time, and on the post-test she checked it is *always* better. However, there are other significant changes as well. For item 5, she now indicates that she *never* feels that the divorce can be the children's fault. Also, instead of *usually* feeling sad and angry about the divorce, she checked that now she *sometimes* does. In the last few sessions, she had begun talking about the possibility of her parents' getting back together if her mom would stop drinking. It seemed like she finally admitted to herself the actual reason for the separation; if just one little thing could change, she rationalized, they could get back together. Notice, she moved from thinking that her parents would never get back together, to now *sometimes* thinking they would.

A HAPPY MARRIAGE
by Lisa

Celebrating a birthday together.

Wife

Husband

IDEAS ABOUT DIVORCE
Post-test by Lisa

Directions: Check to show how you feel at this time.

	NEVER	SOMETIMES	USUALLY	ALWAYS
1. Divorce is a very bad experience.			X	
2. When people marry, they should stay married.		X		
3. Divorce is better than having parents argue all the time.				X
4. Life stays pretty much the same for kids after the divorce as it was before the divorce.			X	
5. When parents get divorced, it can be the children's fault.	X			
6. I like visiting the parent I don't live with.				X
7. I can talk about the divorce with my parents, relatives, or friends and they will listen and understand me.				X
8. Parents should get married again after a divorce, to someone new.	X			
9. I think my parents will get back together again.		X		
10. I feel sad and angry about the divorce.		X		

CASE STUDY OF A SECOND-GRADE BOY

Karl, a second grader, is presently living with his mother and a younger sister. Mother reported that she requested the separation from her husband six months prior to the initial group session, but that father did not actually leave the home until five months later. For Karl, when he started the group, the marital breakup was a recent affair.

In mother's words, the separation "was coming for a long time." She said she and her spouse were married when they were both very young, and both of them changed and grew apart. Mother said that this was her decision, and that dad did not want to separate.

Mother said she and her husband sat down with the children to explain what was happening prior to dad's leaving. Karl cried then and continued to cry afterwards. The children visit dad every weekend. In addition, at first he was coming over every night when it was the children's bedtime to tuck them in and say goodnight. Later on, mother requested that this stop.

Both parents are now dating other people. According to mother, the children like and get along well with the man she is dating, but haven't met dad's new girlfriend.

At first, Karl was reserved. In the first session, when asked to tell something about the family situation, he said, "My mom and dad are getting divorced." During check-in of the third session, he told the group that he saw dad that weekend. Nothing more. Gradually his expression and feelings began to open up. During the seventh session, several months later, when asked how he learned of the divorce and how he felt, he said, "I heard mom say she'd leave. I heard them fighting and it woke me up. I felt sad. I didn't know they'd be breaking up." When asked during the check-in of the eighth session about his week, he talked about how dad was going to pick him up from grandma's house today and take him out to dinner.

Ideas About Divorce Pretest

In item 6, Karl indicates the strong feeling of pleasure he derives when visiting with dad. In item 3, he checked that he *usually* feels divorce is better than having parents argue all the time. Throughout the course of the group, he returns to this issue of arguments. It is probably why, only a month after the separation, he can say that he *never* thinks his parents will get back together again.

IDEAS ABOUT DIVORCE
Pretest by Karl

Directions: Check to show how you feel at this time.

	NEVER	SOMETIMES	USUALLY	ALWAYS
1. Divorce is a very bad experience.				X
2. When people marry, they should stay married.			X	
3. Divorce is better than having parents argue all the time.			X	
4. Life stays pretty much the same for kids after the divorce as it was before the divorce.	X			
5. When parents get divorced, it can be the children's fault.	X			
6. I like visiting the parent I don't live with.				X
7. I can talk about the divorce with my parents, relatives, or friends and they will listen and understand me.				X
8. Parents should get married again after a divorce, to someone new.		X		
9. I think my parents will get back together again.	X			
10. I feel sad and angry about the divorce.		X		

Family Album

A Happy Time with My Family. Before his sister was born, Karl was with mom and dad and they were cutting down trees. This is a typical family togetherness scene.

An Unhappy Time with My Family. Karl's picture shows mom and dad sending him to bed. Dad was leaving him each evening at bedtime. He was probably feeling the loss and separation intensely at this time.

Why I Think My Parents Got Married. Karl said it was because they loved each other. His picture shows them behind a gate with a post between them.

Why I Think My Parents Got Separated. Karl's picture shows mom with someone else "she liked better."

How I Want the Future to Be in My Family. Instead of the typical reunification fantasy that most children draw, Karl drew a picture of mom yelling. In his words, in the future, he would like "mom to stop yelling at my dad."

FAMILY ALBUM
by Karl

A Happy Time with My Family

An Unhappy Time with My Family

Why I Think My Parents Got
Married

Why I Think My Parents Got
Separated/Divorced

How I Want the Future to Be
in My Family

206

Changes

In the first session, on the pretest, Karl checked that life *never* stays the same after a parental breakup. Here, instead of circling the one change that was the most upsetting, Karl circled three: having to live in two different places, having less money, and moving to another house or apartment. The latter two are usually related.

Typically, being eight, he can favorably accept the new partner of his parent. He is clearly a boy who is used to having a strong family support system.

People Who Live in My House

Karl drew small, fragile people on spindly legs without feet, except for himself and his mother, who don't take up much space on the page. In his picture of gram and dad on the worksheet, "Family Members Who Don't Live with Me," the figures are even smaller. This usually indicates feelings of low self-esteem.

CHANGES
by Karl

Having less money	Moving to another house or apartment	Being alone or with a babysitter more because parent needs to work	Having to live in two different places
Having more arguments or fights with brothers and sisters	Spending more time with a parent	Having more responsibilities	Having a parent date or fall in love with someone else
			Seeing a family counselor

208

PEOPLE WHO LIVE IN MY HOUSE
by Karl

FAMILY MEMBERS WHO DON'T LIVE WITH ME
by Karl

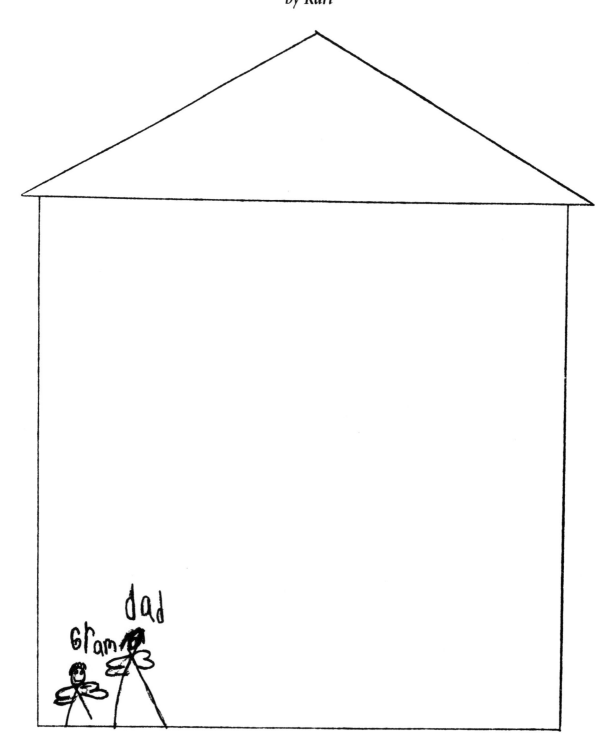

The Grieving Process

At this point, Karl is much more open and in touch with his feelings. His concerns about the arguing crop up very strongly. Here, he is confused about what they argue about, and he has two circles of hope to wish the arguments would stop.

Sadness is the most predominant feeling of children this age. Karl's sadness circle is the largest, and it deals mostly with missing dad. He is realistic about the parental breakup, and accepts the fact that he will live with mom or dad, but not with both together. Also, for the first time, he is able to express anger about it.

A Happy Marriage

Karl did not choose either of his parents and their new partners to illustrate a happy couple. Instead he chose neighbors taking a walk on the beach together.

THE GRIEVING PROCESS
by Karl

Sadness—dad can't come over during the week

Anger—Dad and mom are breaking up

Confused—didn't know what mom and dad argued about.

Hope—mom won't argue with dad anymore.

Acceptance—I will live with my mom or dad—but not with both together.

A HAPPY MARRIAGE
by Karl

Walking at the Beach

Ideas About Divorce Post-test

Karl's feelings seem to be opening up. On the pretest, he indicated he *sometimes* feels sad and angry about the divorce, whereas on the post-test he says he *usually* does. When the shock and denial phase of the grieving process passes, it allows many other feelings to come to the surface.

Karl seems to be accepting the separation more. On the pretest, he responded that divorce is *always* a bad experience, whereas on the post-test he said it *sometimes* is. On the pretest he checked that life never stays the same for kids after a separation or divorce, but on the post-test he said it usually does.

IDEAS ABOUT DIVORCE
Post-test by Karl

Directions: Check to show how you feel at this time.

	NEVER	SOMETIMES	USUALLY	ALWAYS
1. Divorce is a very bad experience.		X		
2. When people marry, they should stay married.			X	
3. Divorce is better than having parents argue all the time.				X
4. Life stays pretty much the same for kids after the divorce as it was before the divorce.			X	
5. When parents get divorced, it can be the children's fault.	X			
6. I like visiting the parent I don't live with.				X
7. I can talk about the divorce with my parents, relatives, or friends and they will listen and understand me.		X		
8. Parents should get married again after a divorce, to someone new.			X	
9. I think my parents will get back together again.		X		
10. I feel sad and angry about the divorce.			X	

• APPENDIX •

Anderson, Penny S. *A Pretty Good Team*. The Child's World, Inc., 1979. 32 p.

Jeff is upset by his parents' constant arguing. Then he learns they are divorcing and that father is moving out of state.

Berger, Terry. *A Friend Can Help*. Raintree Editions, 1974. 32 p.

A grade-school girl shares her feelings about her divorced parents with a friend when her dad takes her to visit.

Berger, Terry. *How Does It Feel When Your Parents Get Divorced?* Julian Messner, Inc., 1977. 62 p.

A girl describes her feelings about her parents' divorce and the changes it makes in her life. After two years, the girl is shown finally accepting the divorce and going on with her life.

Boegehold, Betty. *Daddy Doesn't Live Here Anymore*. Western Publishing Co., 1985.

Casey comes home to find her dad gone. She experiences stomach upsets and she runs away. She even feels it's her fault until both parents reassure her of their love.

Dragonwagon, Crescent. *Always, Always*. Macmillan Publishing Co., Inc., 1984. 32 p.

A girl spends summers with her father in his cabin in Colorado and the rest of the year with her mother in an apartment in New York City. She realizes how different they are from each other and why the marriage didn't work.

Girard, Linda Walvoord. *At Daddy's on Saturdays*. A. Whitman, 1987.

Katie's dad moves out but promises to see Katie on Saturday. During the week preceding the visit, Katie experiences sadness, heaviness, daydreaming at school, loss of appetite, quarreling with her best friend, confusion, feeling at fault. Then, after spending pleasant times with dad on many Saturdays, she begins to accept both parents' houses as home.

Goff, Beth. *Where Is Daddy? The Story of a Divorce*. Beacon Press, 1969. 25 p.

A young girl wakes up to find her father gone. She thinks it's her fault.

Hazen, Barbara Shook. *Two Homes to Live In: A Child's-Eye View of Divorce*. Human Sciences Press, 1978. 40 p.

A boy describes his parents' divorce after their bitter argument and his subsequent feelings of rejection, grief, and anger. His parents continue to show love for him, and eventually he feels content with the good things he does with each parent.

Helmering, Doris Wild. *I Have Two Families*. Abingdon Press, 1981. 46 p.

Eight-year-old Patty tells about life in each of her homes. She and her brother have many fears and anxieties following the divorce, but this book shows how she adjusts happily.

Hogan, Paula Z. *Will Dad Ever Move Back Home?* Raintree Children's Books, 1980. 31 p.

Nine-year-old Laura is very affected by her parents' divorce, and she feels no one will listen or understand her. She runs away and her parents, realizing how unhappy she's been, talk with her and agree to individually spend more time with her.

Lexau, Joan M. *Emily and the Klunky Baby and the Next-Door Dog*. Dial Press, Inc., 1972. 41 p.

Emily's mother, busy with extra responsibilities since the divorce, has Emily look after her younger brother. Emily feels rejected and tries to run away to her father's house.

Lexau, Joan M. *Me Day*. Dial Press, Inc., 1971. 29 p.

A boy is disappointed because he thinks his father, who is divorced from his mother, forgets his birthday. But his dad surprises him with a visit. The book tells about the events that led to the divorce.

Lisker, Sonia Olson and Leigh Dean. *Two Special Cards*. Harcourt Brace Jovanovich, Inc., 1976. 48 p.

Hazel Cooper hears her parents arguing and in the morning, her father is gone. She visits him on the weekend and is comforted.

Paris, Lena. *Mom Is Single*. Children's Press, Inc., 1980. 31 p.

A boy reflects on the difficult changes in his life since his parents divorced.

Perry, Patricia and Marietta Lynch. *Mommy and Daddy Are Divorced*. Dial Press, Inc., 1978. 30 p.

Ned and his brother live with their mother, and dad visits once each week. When dad is about to leave, Ned loses his temper. Dad reassures him. Ned and his mother discuss why she and Ned's dad decided to divorce.

Rogers, Helen Spelman. *Morris and His Brave Lion*. McGraw-Hill Book Co., 1975. 45 p.

Morris, four years old, experiences his parents' arguing and his dad leaving. To help him cope, dad gives Morris a lion, which is strong and courageous. Many changes occur in Morris' life as a result of the divorce.

Schuchman, Joan. *Two Places to Sleep*. Carolrhoda Books, Inc., 1979. 31 p.

David spends weekends with mother, weekdays with father, but he keeps hoping his parents will reunite. Because he feels he may be at fault, he wonders if being good will cause his parents to get back together. In the end, he is better able to accept having two places to sleep.

Simon, Norma. *I Wish I Had My Father*. A. Whitman, 1983. 32 p.

A young boy hates Father's Day because his teachers always want the students to make presents for their fathers. He has no contact with his father. Instead, he makes a card for his grandpa and friends.

MEDIA RESOURCES ABOUT PARENTS DIVORCING

Learning Tree Publishing, Inc. "Coping with Your Parents' Divorce." Englewood, CO. (4 Filmstrips, 4 Cassettes) Gr. 4-8.

Separation, divorce and remarriage are presented through the stories of the lives of various children.

Learning Tree Publishing, Inc. "A Kid's Guide to Divorce." Englewood, CO. (4 Filmstrips, 4 Cassettes or 36-Minute Videocassette) Gr. K-3.

Separation, divorce, and remarriage are addressed.

Paramount. "When Mom and Dad Break Up." Hollywood, CA. (32-Minute Videocassette) Gr. K-6.

Answers questions children of divorced parents have, such as, was the divorce their fault. Also reassures them that their feelings are natural and acceptable.

Ready Reference Press. "20 Helpful Tips for Children of Divorce." Santa Monica, CA. (26-Minute Videocassette) Gr. K-6.

Helping kids cope with the trauma of their parents' divorce is the focus of this video: the emotional upheaval, ways to compensate, and more.

Ready Reference Press. "The Kid's Guide to Surviving Divorce." Santa Monica, CA. (23-Minute Videocassette) Gr. K-6.

The video shows that divorce is not the kids' fault, it is not something they can change, and that there are many confusing feelings they may have.

Sunburst Communications. "When Your Mom and Dad Get Divorced." Pleasantville, NY. (14-Minute Videocassette) Gr. 2-4.

The video uses a true-to-life scenario and upbeat song to demonstrate ways for kids to cope with their negative emotions and see their situation in a more positive light.

Sunburst Communications. "We're a Family." Pleasantville, NY. (15-Minute Videocassette) Gr. 2-4.

The video shows that families come in many different forms, from nuclear to blended to step to single parent, that it is people who care for and about you and offer security and love.

BOOKS ABOUT REMARRIAGE

Drescher, Joan E. *My Mother's Getting Married*. Dial Press, Inc., 1986. 32 p.

Kathy's mother is getting remarried, and she is afraid her mother will love her less and will stop doing things with her. She attends mother's wedding and is reassured.

Shyer, Marlene Fanta. *Stepdog*. Charles Scribner's Sons, 1983. 30 p.

Terry's father remarries Marilyn. Marilyn's dog is jealous of Terry. In this book, the dog has the adjustment problems.

Sobol, Harriet Langsam. *My Other-Mother, My Other-Father*. Macmillan Publishing Co., Inc., 1979.

Twelve-year-old Andrea has two families. Her mother is remarried to Larry, her father to Sharon. She realizes there are good things and bad things about having two families.

Stenson, Janet Sinberg. *Now I Have a Stepparent and It's Kind of Confusing*. Avon, 1979.

Vigna, Judith. *She's Not My Real Mother*. A. Whitman, 1980. 32 p.

Miles is afraid that if he likes his stepmother, he will betray his natural mother. The former is very nice to him, and Miles realizes he can be friends with her.

MEDIA RESOURCES ABOUT REMARRIAGE

Learning Tree Publishing, Inc. "Coping With Your Parents' Divorce." Englewood, CO. (4 Filmstrips and 4 Cassettes) Gr. 4-6.

One of these filmstrips deals entirely with parents' remarriage. Two vignettes are shown starring older elementary-school-aged girls.

Learning Tree Publishing, Inc. "A Kid's Guide to Divorce." Englewood, CO. (4 Filmstrips and 4 Cassettes or a 36-Minute Videocassette) Gr. K-3.

BIBLIOGRAPHY

Diamond, Susan Arnsberg. *Helping Children of Divorce.* Schocken Books: New York, 1985.

Francke, Linda Bird. *Growing Up Divorced.* Linden Press/Simon & Schuster: New York, 1983.

Gardner, Richard A. *The Boys and Girls Book About Divorce.* Science House: New York, 1970.

Gardner, Richard A. *Psychotherapy with Children of Divorce.* Jason Aronson, Inc.: New York, 1976.

Garigan, Elizabeth, and Michael Urbanski. *Living with Divorce: Activities to Help Children Cope with Difficult Situations.* Good Apple: Carthage, IL, 1991.

Hammond, Janice M. *Group Counseling for Children of Divorce: A Guide for the Elementary School.* Cranbrook Publishing Co.: Flint, MI, 1981.

Heegaard, Marge. "When a Parent Marries Again," *Drawing Out Feelings.* Woodland Press: Minneapolis, MN, 1992.

Heegaard, Marge. "When Mom and Dad Separate," *Drawing Out Feelings.* Woodland Press, Minneapolis, MN, 1992.

Ives, Sally Blakeslee, David Fassler, and Michael Lash. *The Divorce Workbook: A Guide for Kids and Families.* Waterfront Books: Burlington, VT, 1985.

Kuhn, Mary Ann. *Coming to Terms with Divorce: A Guided Support Program for Primary Grades.* The Center for Learning, 1992.

LeShan, Eda. *What's Going to Happen to Me? When Parents Separate or Divorce.* Four Winds Press: New York, 1978.

Teyber, Edward. *Helping Children Cope with Divorce.* Lexington Books: New York, 1992.

Wallerstein, Judith S. "Children of Divorce: The Psychological Tasks of the Child." Talk presented at the annual meeting of the American Orthopsychiatric Association, San Francisco, 1982.

Wallerstein, Judith S., and Sandra Blakeslee. *The Good Marriage: How and Why Love Lasts*. Houghton Mifflin Co.: New York, 1995.

Wallerstein, Judith S., and Sandra Blakeslee. *Second Chances: Men, Women, and Children a Decade After Divorce*. Ticknor & Fields: New York, 1989.